Understanding
World History

Ancient
Chinese
Dynasties

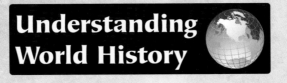
Understanding
World History

Ancient Chinese Dynasties

Cindy Jenson-Elliott

Bruno Leone
Series Consultant

ReferencePoint Press®

San Diego, CA

For more information, contact:
ReferencePoint Press, Inc.
PO Box 27779
San Diego, CA 92198
www.ReferencePointPress.com

LIBRARY OF CONGRESS CATALOGING-IN-PUBLICATION DATA

Jenson-Elliott, Cynthia L.
  Ancient Chinese dynasties / by Cindy Jenson-Elliott.
    pages cm. -- (Understanding world history)
  Audience: Grade 9 to 12.
  Includes bibliographical references and index.
  ISBN 978-1-60152-738-7 (hardback) -- ISBN 1-60152-738-1 (hardback)
1. China--Kings and rulers--History--Juvenile literature. 2. Royal houses--China--History--Juvenile literature. 3. China--History--221 B.C-960 A.D.--Juvenile literature. 4. China--History--960–1644--Juvenile literature. I. Title.
  DS747.38.J46   2015
  951--dc23

                            2014013326

Contents

Foreword

When the Puritans first emigrated from England to America in 1630, they believed that their journey was blessed by a covenant between themselves and God. By the terms of that covenant they agreed to establish a community in the New World dedicated to what they believed was the true Christian faith. God, in turn, would reward their fidelity by making certain that they and their descendants would always experience his protection and enjoy material prosperity. Moreover, the Lord guaranteed that their land would be seen as a shining beacon—or in their words, a "city upon a hill"—that the rest of the world would view with admiration and respect. By embracing this notion that God could and would shower his favor and special blessings upon them, the Puritans were adopting the providential philosophy of history—meaning that history is the unfolding of a plan established or guided by a higher intelligence.

The concept of intercession by a divine power is only one of many explanations of the driving forces of world history. Historians and philosophers alike have subscribed to numerous other ideas. For example, the ancient Greeks and Romans argued that history is cyclical. Nations and civilizations, according to these ancients of the Western world, rise and fall in unpredictable cycles; the only certainty is that these cycles will persist throughout an endless future. The German historian Oswald Spengler (1880–1936) echoed the ancients to some degree in his controversial study *The Decline of the West*. Spengler asserted that all civilizations inevitably pass through stages comparable to the life span of a person: childhood, youth, adulthood, old age, and, eventually, death. As the title of his work implies, Western civilization is currently entering its final stage.

Joining those who see purpose and direction in history are thinkers who completely reject the idea of meaning or certainty. Rather, they reason that since there are far too many random and unseen factors at work on the earth, historians would be unwise to endorse historical predictability of any type. Warfare (both nuclear and conventional), plagues, earthquakes, tsunamis, meteor showers, and other catastrophic world-changing events have loomed large throughout history and prehistory. In his essay "A Free Man's Worship," philosopher and mathematician

Bertrand Russell (1872–1970) supported this argument, which many refer to as the nihilist or chaos theory of history. According to Russell, history follows no preordained path. Rather, the earth itself and all life on earth resulted from, as Russell describes it, an "accidental collocation of atoms." Based on this premise, he pessimistically concluded that all human achievement will eventually be "buried beneath the debris of a universe in ruins."

Whether history does or does not have an underlying purpose, historians, journalists, and countless others have nonetheless left behind a record of human activity tracing back nearly 6,000 years. From the dawn of the great ancient Near Eastern civilizations of Mesopotamia and Egypt to the modern economic and military behemoths China and the United States, humanity's deeds and misdeeds have been and continue to be monitored and recorded. The distinguished British scholar Arnold Toynbee (1889–1975), in his widely acclaimed twelve-volume work entitled *A Study of History*, studied twenty-one different civilizations that have passed through history's pages. He noted with certainty that others would follow.

In the final analysis, the academic and journalistic worlds mostly regard history as a record and explanation of past events. From a more practical perspective, history represents a sequence of building blocks—cultural, technological, military, and political—ready to be utilized and enhanced or maligned and perverted by the present. What that means is that all societies—whether advanced civilizations or preliterate tribal cultures—leave a legacy for succeeding generations to either embrace or disregard.

Recognizing the richness and fullness of history, the ReferencePoint Press Understanding World History series fosters an evaluation and interpretation of history and its influence on later generations. Each volume in the series approaches its subject chronologically and topically, with specific focus on nations, periods, or pivotal events. Primary and secondary source quotations are included, along with complete source notes and suggestions for further research.

Moreover, the series reflects the truism that the key to understanding the present frequently lies in the past. With that in mind, each series title concludes with a legacy chapter that highlights the bonds between past and present and, more important, demonstrates that world history is a continuum of peoples and ideas, sometimes hidden but there nonetheless, waiting to be discovered by those who choose to look.

Important Events of the Ancient Chinese Dynasties

ca. 1600
The Shang Dynasty leaves first-known written records of a dynasty in scratches etched on the shoulder bones of cattle.

ca. 500
Confucius is born into a poor branch of an aristocratic family and goes on to become an ordinary clerk, then an extraordinary teacher.

ca. 200
The Han Dynasty creates the first of China's great walls by joining sections of smaller walls together.

213
Qin Shi Huangdi orders the burning of thousands of books and the execution of 460 Confucian scholars.

BCE **1600** ••• **1000** ••• **500** ••• **300**   **200**   **100**

ca. 1050
The Zhou Dynasty overthrows the Shang and goes on to lead China for eight hundred years.

221
Qin Shi Huangdi unifies the many city-states of China and founds the Qin Dynasty.

138
Emperor Wudi sends Zhang Qian in search of new markets and military exploits, a venture that spurs Silk Road trade between China and the West.

206
The Han Dynasty overthrows Qin Shi Huangdi's successor; historian Sima Qian begins writing the first great history of China.

ca. 220
The Han Dynasty ends, heralding four hundred years of unrest in China; Buddhism becomes established and spreads throughout China.

1274
Italian merchant Marco Polo arrives in China; more than a century later, his journals recounting his experiences are published in Europe, spurring interest in China.

1127
Expansion of the Grand Canal creates new markets for goods and allows the Song Dynasty to expand.

907
Unrest in China lasting two generations divides the nation into brief dynasties and several kingdoms known as the five dynasties and ten kingdoms period.

CE **200 ••• 600   800   1000   1200   1400**

618
The Tang Dynasty is established.

960
The Song Dynasty begins its rule of China.

1211
The Mongols, led by Genghis Khan and later by his grandson, Kublai Khan, begin nearly seventy years of rule in China.

1271
Mongol leader Kublai Khan establishes the Yuan Dynasty; he takes a Chinese name.

1368
The Ming Dynasty overthrows the Mongols, reestablishing Han Chinese traditions and building significant portions of the Great Wall and constructing the Forbidden City.

The Defining Characteristics of the Ancient Chinese Dynasties

When the first Europeans visited China in the 1500s, they sent back descriptions of majesty that defied belief. Matteo Ricci, a Jesuit missionary, described seeing a floating convoy more than 2 miles (3 km) long on the Grand Canal. The convoy, transporting wood to rebuild a burned palace, was pulled by tens of thousands of workers. Such was the power of a Chinese dynasty, or ruling family. Chinese dynasties commanded the work of multitudes and the wealth of nations. Written records, paintings, sculptures, and tapestries created over three millennia ago leave behind a detailed history of the power, extravagance, and achievement of China's dynasties.

Emperors were powerful because they controlled the lives of their subjects. At the emperor's command, millions of peasants built roads, walls, canals, and palaces. And if an emperor needed attendants in the afterlife, followers were expected to serve there as well. The ramp to the Shang Dynasty burial chambers, for example, was filled with the beheaded bodies of dozens of imperial followers.

With power came extravagance. Court records show that tailors for Emperor Wan Li, who ruled from 1572 to 1620, spent thirteen years creating an embroidered ceremonial robe and a black cap studded with golden dragons and jewels as big as almonds. Such extravagance extended not only to the emperor but also to his enormous entourage. Wan Li's Ming Dynasty court, for example, included more than thirty-three thousand people—ministers and subministers, concubines and eunuchs, soldiers, workers, and artisans.

The wealth of China's dynasties supported an extravagant lifestyle as well as a sophisticated society. At a time when people in many parts of the world were still living in mud huts, China's dynastic scholars were writing tracts of philosophy, Chinese thinkers produced inventions such as paper, explosives, and crossbows, and Chinese engineers built large and lasting public works projects, including walls, canals, palaces, and tombs.

A multitude of dynasties ruled China from about 1760 BCE to the early 1900s CE, for periods ranging from twenty to eight hundred years. But dynasties did not always succeed each other in a smooth transition. For some long periods, such as the Period of Disunion between 220 and 589 CE, several dynasties ruled simultaneously in different parts of China.

A Mandate from Heaven

The power of China's dynasties rose from the belief that a dynasty's right to lead was divinely given—a mandate from heaven. When a dynasty fell from power and was succeeded by another, the populace understood that this was also due to heavenly mandate.

Emperors, too, shared the belief that they ruled by the grace of heaven. They looked to the heavens for portents, or signs, when making decisions. If they made a mistake, or acted against heaven's wishes, the dynasty could fall from favor. As historian J.A.G. Roberts writes in his *History of China*, "If . . . rulers did not respond to repeated warnings, which took the form of portents, the mandate of heaven was transferred to the founder of a new dynasty."[1] When the last Ming emperor, Chongzhen, lost his throne in 1644, he saw it as a sign of heaven's displeasure. He wrote, "I, feeble and small of stature, have offended against Heaven; the rebels have seized my capital because my ministers deceived me. Shamed to face my ancestors, I die. Removing my imperial cap and with my hair disheveled about my face, I leave to the rebels the dismemberment of my body. Let them not harm my people!"[2]

Cycles of Chaos and Harmony

Despite the belief that heaven decreed the course of history, dynastic succession—the change from one dynasty to another—was rarely calm, bloodless, or quick. Dynastic change was most often characterized by revolving cycles of union and disunion, chaos and harmony, idealism and corruption. As historian Su Shuyang describes it, "Like a meandering and gushing river, the history of China has clearly experienced ups and downs, rapids and reverse flows."[3]

At the start of a new dynasty, the ruler eliminated rivals and put in place a new and promising government. Often that promise eroded as corruption took hold. Powerful families gained more power and more wealth while the poor, who made up the majority of China's population, suffered. Eventually, peasants bore so much of the tax and labor burden that they rebelled and overthrew the dynasty. Thus, the cycle swung into disunion and chaos.

The Characteristics of Chinese Dynasties

The specific characteristics of different dynasties were most influenced by the region and culture from which they sprang. The first dynasties grew out of agricultural regions and cultures in what is now south-central China. These dynasties were characterized by the concerns of settled societies: building walls, irrigating fields, amassing material fortunes, and creating a literate culture. Other dynasties sprang up from largely pastoral, or animal-herding, cultures of the dry north. These cultures brought military endeavor, horsemanship, and arid land management techniques to China. These two types of dynasties represent a significant cultural divide in China: agrarian versus pastoral cultures. This cultural conflict influenced much of Chinese history and resulted in China's most memorable structure—the Great Wall—which was built to separate agrarian communities from pastoral ones.

Regardless of the culture of origin, Chinese dynasties are characterized by a set of defining characteristics that determined their success. These characteristics included military might, administrative

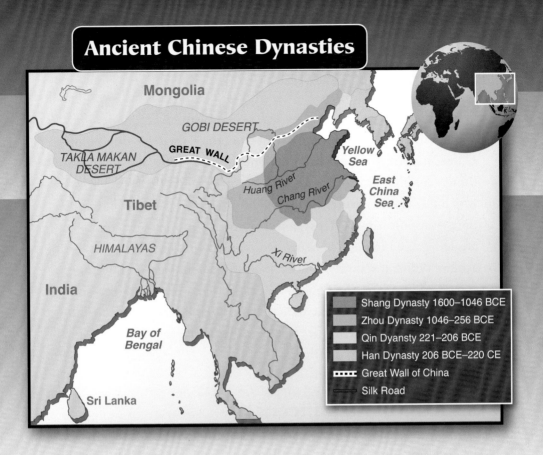

Ancient Chinese Dynasties

Mongolia

GOBI DESERT

TAKLA MAKAN
DESERT

GREAT WALL

Yellow
Sea

Huang River

Chang River

East
China
Sea

Tibet

HIMALAYAS

Xi River

India

Bay of
Bengal

Sri Lanka

	Shang Dynasty 1600–1046 BCE
	Zhou Dynasty 1046–256 BCE
	Qin Dyansty 221–206 BCE
	Han Dynasty 206 BCE–220 CE
▪▪▪▪	Great Wall of China
▭▭	Silk Road

organization, political stability, cultural distinction, and an emperor
who symbolized personal magnificence.

Dynasties generally came to power through a combination of in-
trigue and military endeavor. Imperial and palace plots, the coalescing
of military power, and the ultimate overthrow of a leader were all ele-
ments of change from one dynasty to another. During the scope of a
dynasty, however, military might, taxation, and forced labor were all
used to keep ordinary people under control, expand borders, and widen
a dynasty's regional influence.

Although military skill is useful for expanding an empire and conquering enemies, it does not help leaders run a country. The most suc-
cessful dynasties, therefore, also became skilled administrators. They
developed systems of bureaucracy to make one nation of diverse people
and far-flung geographies.

Public works projects helped unify disparate parts of China. In addition to the well-known Great Wall, dynasties created canal and road systems, tombs and palaces. All of this was done with the forced labor of millions of people who were under the control of the emperor.

Standardization helped dynasties organize their far-flung empire. Different parts of China had different ways of doing just about everything. Unifying diverse communities meant standardizing every way in which the diverse parts of China might interact, including communication, transportation, defense, and commerce. In many ways, dynasties created one China out of many. Standardization also helped dynasties achieve political stability. Once a dynasty took power, set up a bureaucracy to administer the nation, and expanded and maintained control through military might, the nation could be politically stable for a long time. In fact, some dynasties lasted as long as eight hundred years before being replaced by another.

Style and Magnificence

Dynasties were characterized by their styles of art and culture as well. Practices such as foot binding, hairstyles such as the queue, philosophies such as Confucianism, and arts such as brushwork, poetry, and ceramics can be identified as characteristic of particular dynastic periods and of the personal magnificence of the emperors themselves.

Many emperors left behind monuments glorifying their reigns. Using the forced labor of China's huge population, emperors created opulent palaces, tombs, and cities. Convinced that their mandate to rule was from heaven, dynastic leaders often assumed their leadership rights would extend to the afterlife. They left behind tombs filled with statues of soldiers, stonework armor, clothing and jewels, and mountains of food to help them survive and thrive in the afterlife.

Chinese dynasties have left behind treasures that continue to influence China and the world at large. In modern bureaucracies and systems for organizing society, philosophical and religious beliefs, art and crafts, scientific and mathematical discoveries and inventions, China's enduring dynastic legacy lives on.

Chapter 1

What Conditions Led to the Ancient Chinese Dynasties?

Archaeological evidence reveals that China has been occupied for five hundred thousand years. In the 1940s archaeologists discovered a skeleton of an early hominid—an early relative of humans—that came to be known as Peking Man. Since then, archaeological evidence, written history, and ancient myth have come together to form an increasingly detailed picture of China's ancient past.

In the mesolithic period, seminomadic people wandered China's central plains and river valleys. They gathered wild-growing foods, fished in the region's many rivers, and hunted animal herds. Over time, their hunting-gathering lifestyle changed. In a part of central China known as the Han cradle of civilization, hunting-gathering people began to practice swidden, or shifting, agriculture, which is the practice of clearing trees, rocks, and unwanted plants off of a piece of land to plant food crops. When the land lost its vitality, the farmers moved on and cleared a new piece of land, letting the first return to its natural state. By 5000 BCE the people of the Han cradle farmed throughout the region, leaving behind decorated pottery, jade, and carved bone and tortoiseshell fragments.

Controlling Water

By 2500 BCE the people of central China had begun to settle into permanent agricultural communities near the Wei, Yangtze, and Yellow Rivers. The rivers provided the farmers with rich, fertile soil and a moist, moderate climate, but flooding was common. People began to live together in larger communities to help each other with the intense labor of farming—especially controlling water. Communities dug channels to divert flood water from fields and to irrigate crops. Historian Owen Lattimore describes how this control of water drew people together, creating a changed landscape and a "hydaulic civilization." He says, "The control of soil and water in combination lay only within the reach of groups of people helping each other to dig larger channels and perhaps to build embankments that would keep flood water out of bottom lands."[4] Controlling water led to increased crop yields and food surpluses. Historians believe that these surpluses may have led to the first differences in wealth and power among people of the region. People who could store surplus food were more wealthy and powerful than those who could not. These gradations of wealth may have led to the formation of the first dynasties and the emergence of civilization in China.

By the second millennium BCE the Han cradle held thousands of agricultural settlements. As the population expanded, powerful groups pushed weaker peoples north into an arid landscape unsuited to farming. The people pushed into these high-altitude steppes depended on animals such as sheep, goats and small Mongolian horses for milk, meat, skins and wool. As the climate of the north became drier, the people of this region left agriculture behind completely and became nomadic and pastoral—mobile animal herders, hunters, and warriors. These were the legendary wild horsemen of the north, in conflict with China throughout history.

Mythology Meets Archaeology

China's legendary history is as rich as that which is documented. Stories passed down over millennia tell of not only the wild horsemen of the north but also of the earliest people in China, the roots of society,

The fertile Yangtze River valley, pictured in recent times, was the site of some of the earliest agricultural settlements in China. Inhabitants of the area learned to channel the river for irrigation.

and the origins of the universe. One such story, for example, retold by historian Su Shuyang, reveals the origins of a common Chinese understanding of yin and yang, or balance in the universe:

> In the beginning, all was blackness and emptiness. Then, suddenly, a small bubble appeared. The bubble became a ball of smoke, which then began to coalesce. It grew and grew for a millennia, eventually becoming a red, egg-shaped object.
>
> This was the gestating Pan Gu. After 18,000 years, he awoke. Appalled by the infinite blackness, he threw open his arms and legs to break the suffocating emptiness, separating heaven and earth. . . . The clear and light positive energies (yang) rose gradually, becoming the sky. The turbid and heavy negative energies (yin) descended gradually, becoming the earth.[5]

Sun Tzu and *The Art of War*

During the warring states period, as the military became an organized, permanent force, military specialists offered their expertise to each of the seven states. Among the most famous of these specialists was Sun Tzu, who is assumed to be the author of *The Art of War*, written around 500 BCE. Sun Tzu's advice ranged from small details about the monetary cost of raising an army to psychological insights into warfare. In one passage he clarifies the importance of deception in warfare: "All warfare is based on deception. Hence, when able to attack, we must seem unable; when using our forces, we must seem inactive; when we are near, we must make the enemy believe we are far away; when far away, we must make him believe we are near. Hold out baits to entice the enemy. Feign disorder, and crush him."

Quoted in Sun Tzu, *The Art of War*, Ch.1, in Loyola University–Chicago Chinese Cultural Studies, "The Mandate of Heaven." www.luc.edu/faculty/ldossey/Chinesetexts.htm.

Although origin myths such as this may appear to be fanciful, they often contain a kernel of truth. In Chinese legends, after Pan Gu created the earth, China was governed by a series of wise men who gave humankind inventions, social rules, and institutions. Huangdi, also known as "the Yellow Emperor," is perhaps the best known of the mythological rulers. He brought writing, pottery, and the first calendar to the people. Emperor Yao, who helped China tame its rivers and control floods, was followed by sage rulers Shun and Yu. It is with Yu that China's mythological history merges with written history and archaeology. In 2205 BCE Yu is said to have founded the Xia Dynasty. Having a dynasty, rather than simply a ruler, meant that China could have continuity of leadership.

The Xia Dynasty

Until recently, verifiable evidence of the Xia Dynasty has been slim. The few records of Xia genealogy were found only in the writings of historian Sima Qian, who wrote many centuries after the Xia Dynasty was supposed to have existed. Later, however, the same genealogy was found inscribed on the shoulder bones of animals. Their rudimentary Chinese characters suggested that perhaps the Xia Dynasty may have existed after all.

More recently, scientists have found evidence of settlements in the Yellow River valley dating from between 2070 and 1600 BCE—the period the Xia Dynasty is thought to have existed. Palace-like buildings, tombs, and bronze containers, similar to those of the Erlitou material culture in Henan have been unearthed. *Material culture* is a term meaning all of the material evidence of a culture that has been found, when no other written historical record exists. Because no written record yet exists to link the Erlitou archaeological items with the Xia Dynasty, the Xia Dynasty remains an unsolved mystery—maybe myth, maybe fact.

The Shang Dynasty and Social Hierarchy

The Shang Dynasty is the first dynasty in which archaeological evidence corresponds with a written record. Ruling east-central China between 1600 and 1046 BCE, the Shang Dynasty has been associated with the walled cities of the Erligang material culture of northern China. Archaeological remains, as well as writings carved on turtle shells and the shoulder blades of cattle, provide a glimpse into the Shang's socially stratified society. At the top were the Shang rulers who performed religious ceremonies and rituals, ruled society as administrators, and established relationships with clan leaders in the region. They created new towns and opened land for agriculture. Supporting Shang rulers were aristocratic clans who drove horse chariots and helped the king wage war on neighboring communities as a means to acquiring prisoners and goods. Underneath the nobility were peasants who cleared the land to grow millet. Beneath the peasants were slaves. The king had the right to call on the nobility to fight, and nobles had the right to call on peasants to labor and farm for the king's cause.

Those at the bottom of the social scale served another purpose as well. They were buried in the tombs of kings as human sacrifices. More than ten thousand human sacrifices have been found in Shang burial chambers, often beheaded. Horses were sacrificed too, their bodies laid to rest alongside the humans.

A Bronze Age Culture

Along with the corpses of human and animal sacrifices, Shang tombs included chambers full of important objects made from jade—thought to have spiritual value—and bronze. The use of bronze developed during this period and gained increasing importance during the Shang

The Shang Dynasty is well known for its many bronze objects. The tomb of Fu Hao, a mistress of an ancient Shang king, contained more than two hundred bronze vessels. The tomb is pictured.

Dynasty. For example, the tomb of Fu Hao—a mistress of a Shang king in about 1250 BCE—was found to contain more than two hundred bronze vessels, many in the shape of animals.

Bronze manufacturing developed into an industry during the Shang Dynasty. The production, use, and ownership of bronze were under the control of the king. Metal was extracted from ore and cast in molds in pieces that were then assembled into objects by skilled craftsmen. Bronze objects included wine goblets, ceremonial vessels with tripod legs and monster masks used to drive away evil from burial chambers.

Religious beliefs during this period likely involved the worship of royal ancestral deities—deceased members of the royal family who took on the status of gods. The Shang also may have worshipped other deities, such as nature spirits and mythological gods. Some historians believe that the Shang had a supreme god called Di, who was in charge of all the other gods. But other historians believe that the Shang term *di* simply referred to all the gods together as a group.

The Legacy of the Shang Dynasty

The history of the Shang Dynasty has been pieced together over time from a variety of clues including oracle bones used in fortune-telling. To create oracle bones, diviners—people who could read the future—applied a hot poker to cattle bones or turtle shells while chanting a prayer, request, or question. When the bones cracked, diviners looked at the crack patterns to determine the answer to their questions or discover the future. They called this practice crack-making. They then carved a record of the event into the bone. Many inscriptions were records of offerings to Di.

More than two hundred thousand pieces of bone, dating from 1250 to 1192 BCE, have been found around Xiaotun. The following inscription, made around 1200 BCE, consists of opposing prophecies on different sides of a bone: "Crack-making on jiashen [day 1] Zheng divined: 'This rain will be disastrous for us.' 'This rain will not be disastrous for us.'"[6] On other bones, inscriptions record ordinary events such as weather, agriculture, or information about royalty, military alliances, and the organization of the government. Together, collections of oracle bones offer evidence of China's first complex governmental, religious, and ancestral hierarchies as well as the importance of fortune telling in ancient Chinese culture.

The Rise of the Zhou Dynasty

While the Shang Dynasty is the best-known Bronze Age culture of China, it was not the only culture living in central China during the second millennium BCE. Toward the end of the Shang Dynasty, another culture gained power and interacted with the Shang: the Zhou. The Zhou ultimately replaced the Shang as rulers of China.

The Zhou Dynasty is the longest dynasty in the history of China; it held power for about eight hundred years, dating from about 1046 to 256 BCE. In many ways the Zhou were similar to the Shang. They

An inscription, carved long ago in this Shang Dynasty oracle bone, provides a record of an important event. Such bones provide evidence of China's early traditions and ways of life.

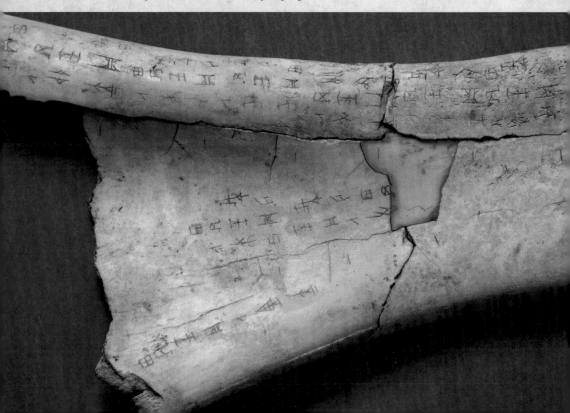

ruled a larger area of east-central China, but the Zhou resembled the Shang linguistically, culturally, and administratively. Both believed that dynasties rose and fell as a result of heaven's mandate. One of China's earliest historical records from the Zhou period, the *Shujing,* or *Book of Documents,* acknowledges this belief:

> Oh! do you, who now succeed to the throne, revere these warnings in your person. Think of them!—sacred counsels of vast importance, admirable words forcibly set forth! The ways of Heaven are not invariable:—on the good-doer it sends down all blessings, and on the evil-doer it sends down all miseries. Do you but be virtuous, be it in small things or in large, and the myriad regions will have cause for rejoicing. If you not be virtuous, be it in large things or in small, it will bring the ruin of your ancestral temple.[7]

The Zhou Establish New Traditions

While the Zhou Dynasty was similar to the Shang, historians note some important differences between the two. Whereas the Shang Dynasty passed dynastic leadership from brother to brother, the Zhou passed leadership from father to son. In addition, many historians believe that Zhou society was feudal. In a feudal society, a king grants land—a fiefdom—to regional lords. These lords then promise military loyalty to the king, while peasants pledge their loyalty and labor to the lord. This was the structure of early Zhou society. Unlike Europe's feudal societies, however, Zhou titles were not hereditary and could be revoked at any time.

As Zhou territory expanded through military conquest, enormous changes began to take place in society. For one thing, use of bronze agricultural tools expanded, making food more abundant and available. With better nutrition, the population grew and the economy transformed. In 594 BCE, for example, leaders of Lu, an independent state within the Zhou, demanded that peasants pay taxes. With taxes, a free market developed in which goods were traded for other goods. Not long afterward metallic coins, in the form of knives and spades, began

Confucianism

onfucius lived around 551 to 479 BCE. He traveled widely, sharing his wisdom and writing his views on life. Confucius believed there had been a golden age in Chinese history, long before his own time, when kings and leaders were *jen*, or "benevolent," and behaved in an exemplary moral and ethical manner. He called on the current leaders of states to follow the examples of the past and become *junzi*, "princely" men. By showing proper respect for ancestors and those of higher rank and by cultivating good manners and intellectual and moral understanding, individuals could become *junzi*.

Confucius's teachings were designed to help individuals develop virtue and moral understanding within themselves and society and to help society run smoothly through a system of traditions and manners that everyone could practice together. In his most famous work, the *Analects*, Confucius explains to a questioning student how individual development relates to a well-ordered society:

"He cultivates himself and thereby achieves reverence."

"Is that all?"

"He cultivates himself and thereby brings peace and security to his fellow men."

"Is that all?"

"He cultivates himself and thereby brings peace and security to the people."

Quoted in J.A.G. Roberts, *A History of China*. 3rd ed. London: Palgrave MacMillan, 2011, p. 16.

to take the place of goods in trade. A modern economy was appearing.

With wealth, however, came conflict. Leaders of individual fiefdoms became wealthier and more independent. Finally, the king appointed so many fiefdoms—170 in all—that he began to lose control. Fiefdoms became more like independent states with only nominal allegiance to the king.

Between 771 and 481 BCE conflict between states was frequent. By 475, 170 states had been whittled down to seven: Qi, Chu, Yan, Han, Zhao, Wei, and Qin. Conflict became a way of life. States created weapons of iron, standing armies of six hundred thousand men, and walled cities to keep enemies out. Conflict grew between Chinese and non-Chinese people, too, as farmers pushed north to turn arid lands into farms. Amid this era of war, one state began to grow in power, influenced by both the north and the south. Qin was about to change Chinese society forever.

Chapter 2

Unity Under Empire: The Qin and Han Dynasties

In 400 BCE, Qin was among the least developed of the seven warring states. Han, Chu, and Wei in the central and southern plains, and Yan, Zhao, and Qi in the north were more prosperous economically, and more developed politically and culturally than Qin, the backward state of the northwest. But that was about to change.

Living on China's northwest border, Qin occupied a transition zone between the farmers of the south and the herders of the north. Qin was influenced by its neighbors on both sides of the border but particularly by the horsemen of the north. Qin was also influenced by another important and growing force in the region: foreign trade. Located along active trade routes between Asia and the Middle East, Qin had a cosmopolitan view of trade and saw trade routes as opportunities to exchange products and personnel with other nations.

In 361 BCE, Duke Xiao of Qin issued an invitation similar to those that might be issued today by prosperous companies seeking to grow: "Any citizen of Qin or foreign visitor who can devise a way to make Qin stronger and more prosperous will be invited to serve in my government."[8] Immigrants flocked to Qin, creating a culturally and economically diverse society.

One such immigrant to Qin was Gangsu Yang, later known as Shang Yang. Shang Yang was a minor government official and nobleman who left a post in Wei, where he had introduced some revolutionary—and not entirely welcome—ideas. Officials in Wei had considered Shang Yang to be very talented but also a threat. They wrote, "If he is not to

The Origins of Emperor Qin Shi Huangdi

King Zheng of Qin, who rose to become Qin Shi Huangdi, the first emperor of China, may not have been the son of the king of Qin at all. Instead, some historians believe he may have been the illegitimate son of a merchant. In the middle of the third century BCE a wealthy and clever merchant named Lu Buwei befriended Zichu, a son of the king of Qin, who had been taken hostage in the state of Zhao. As a sign of friendship, Lu gave Zichu the gift of his favorite concubine, a beautiful woman. The concubine soon bore a son, who was given the name Zheng. Some historians believe the boy was actually Lu's son rather than the son of the Qin prince.

At this time the heir to the Qin throne was childless. Lu traveled to Qin and persuaded the heir to accept Zichu as his heir. Zichu returned to Qin with his concubine and child, and when the Qin ruler and the heir died in quick succession, Zichu became the ruler of Qin. He appointed Lu as his chancellor, or closest adviser. When Zichu died after only three years on the throne, Lu continued on as chancellor, advising the child-king Zheng. Whether Zheng was the legitimate son of Zichu or of Lu, he went on to become China's first emperor, unifying China through military and bureaucratic means.

J.A.G. Roberts, *A History of China*, 3rd ed. London: Palgrave MacMillan, 2011. p. 25–26.

be employed in an official post, it would be better to put him to death, lest another kingdom obtain his services."[9]

Shang Yang's views were controversial because he rejected the Confucian ideas that governed most Chinese states. He believed that rules, rather than traditions, should guide states. His new philosophy was called legalism. Unlike Confucianism, which favored rule of a traditional aristocracy over a landless peasantry, under legalism land no longer would be held by traditional landlords. It would be subject to the free market.

Duke Xiao of Qin liked Shang's unconventional ideas about everything from governance to the economy. In particular, he challenged Qin's adherence to Confucianism. While Confucian practice dictated that society would run smoothly if everyone stuck to traditions, Shang advised Duke Xiao to abandon traditions and offer incentives and punishments for good and bad behavior. "To make a country stronger and more prosperous," Shang wrote,

> attention must be paid to developing agriculture and motivating the military. Good government requires an effective system of incentives and disincentives. If rewards and punishments are perceived to be quick and certain as well as just, the government's authority and credibility will be enhanced and reforms will go through more easily.[10]

Before long, Duke Xiao named Shang as the Qin official in charge of reforming the government and society.

Radical Change

Shang's reforms radically altered Qin society. Basing his changes on the belief that agriculture and the military were the cornerstones of a strong society, Shang set about changing everything from land ownership to taxation to military service. Gone were the Confucian hierarchies that used to determine rank and role in society. In their place, Shang created new rankings and titles based on distinguished military service.

Confucius, whose ideas about tradition and respect guided much of China for centuries, considers a prisoner's plea. During the Qin Dynasty, Shang Yang rejected Confucian ideas in favor of societal rules.

Peasants were no longer subjects in a feudal system, tilling square tracts of soil on behalf of the landed gentry. Shang ordered agricultural boundaries dissolved and rules of ownership changed, enabling peasants and merchants new opportunities for creating businesses. Land ownership, for instance, could be claimed by anyone who worked to enhance and till a piece of land successfully.

In addition to changing agriculture, Shang created new administrative procedures and bureaucratic divisions. Geographic zones called *xian,* which combined cities, towns, and villages into counties, were administered by a new class of public servant: mandarins. Mandarins were appointed by the state to rule over administrative districts and maintain law and order according to a written legal code stating rules and punishments for lawbreakers.

Administrative divisions were also created on a much smaller scale. Agricultural communities were divided into groups of five to ten families who would monitor each other's behavior and productivity. Wrongdoings by one person could result in punishment of the group, and the group was responsible for keeping individual behavior in line. Another of Shang's changes had to do with taxation. In most states peasants labored on behalf of nobles; in Qin, peasants labored for, and paid taxes directly to the king. The population was registered and counted in a census, and taxes were levied for each person. Together, these changes had the effect of taking power away from the nobility and putting power, wealth, and loyalty firmly in the hands of a centralized government. The age of bureaucracy had begun. Over ten years, Shang's reforms led to increased wealth, prosperity, and power in Qin. And with its increased power, Qin began a military campaign to conquer its neighbors.

Qin Expands

Qin's adoption of Shang's legalist guidance set it apart from the other states of the period. In fact, other states roundly criticized Qin for its lack of culture, a cornerstone of Confucian societies. "Qin has the same customs as the Rong and Di barbarians [of the north]," a Wei nobleman wrote in a letter to his king. "It has the heart of a tiger or wolf. It is avaricious, perverse, greedy for profit and . . . knows nothing about etiquette, proper relationships and virtuous conduct."[11]

But what Qin lacked in culture, it more than made up for in military might. All areas of Qin society supported the war effort. Men constituted the fighting force, while women provisioned the army and constructed defenses. Members of society who were too old to fight took care of livestock or harvested food.

As a military power, Qin drew tactics from the so-called barbarians of the north to outwit and outmaneuver enemies. Using swift horse-men, Qin warriors swept down on plodding armies of foot soldiers and heavy chariots. Under this onslaught, the independent states of China fell. The Rong fell to Qin in about 400 BCE. Between 364 and 234 BCE, historians estimate, 1.4 million foreign soldiers and civilians died in Qin wars. One of the most important states to fall was Zhou, whose king was deposed in 256 BCE. One by one, the other states of China succumbed to Qin's might. By 224 BCE Qin had conquered Zhao, Han, and Wei. Chu and Qi fell between 223 and 221 BCE. Writing a hundred years later, Han historian Sima Qian wrote, "As a silkworm devours a mulberry leaf, so Qin swallowed up the kingdoms of the Empire."[12] In 221 BCE King Zheng of Qin declared himself Qin Shi Huangdi, "the First Emperor of Qin." A new era had begun.

Ruling a Unified China

As the new emperor of China, Qin Shi Huangdi set about unifying Chi-nese society and imposing a new bureaucracy throughout his empire. He first set about dismantling the power of the aristocracy throughout the empire. He ordered aristocrats to move with their families to the newly established Qin capital, where he could keep an eye on them. There, their weapons were melted down and made into statues. In ad-dition, Qin Shi Huangdi ordered the walls between and around cities to be knocked down. The empire was now separated into thirty-six dis-tinct divisions, each run by administrators appointed by the emperor's government. In each region, three types of leadership were put into place—one civil, one military, and one supervisory—so that no leader could gain too much power politically, economically, or militarily over the region.

Standardizing the Empire

Unifying so many different states into one nation meant more than just unifying people politically. It meant standardizing diverse economies, languages, and systems of measurement so that people could speak

An army of 7,000 life-size terra-cotta clay soldiers stands guard in the tomb of Qin Shi Huangdi, China's first Qin emperor. The emperor ordered construction of many large projects, including a long portion of the Great Wall of China.

to each other, trade with each other, and work together. According to Sima, Li Si, a politician and legalist philosopher, was charged with bringing about the changes. Applying legalist ideas to the new nation, Li began by creating standardized systems of weights and measures, standardized widths of roads and the axles of carts, and a standardized monetary system of gold and copper coins. Because language had been a barrier to commerce, Li set out to standardize written language. Historians believe that he may have gathered together scholars to develop a standardized script—written pictographs or characters—that would be used universally throughout the empire on official communications. This new standardized script was known as the Small Seal.

Expanding Territory and Public Works Projects

Even after unifying the states into a single nation, Qin Shi Huangdi was not done expanding his empire. The emperor sent military expeditions south and later sent civilians as colonists to set up agricultural communities in what are now Guangdong Province and the Guangxi autonomous region. To reach these areas more easily, he ordered workers to begin digging a canal to join the Yangtze and Pearl river basins in central China.

In the north, where agricultural lands abutted the semiarid plains of the Ordos region, the emperor sent his most famous general, Meng Tian, to drive out the Xiongnu, the nomadic pastoral tribe that lived in the region. Chinese farmers were sent in as colonists to turn pastureland to agricultural purposes in an attempt to gain a foothold in the new territories of the north, and the army attempted to roust the nomads. But military might was not enough to gain a stronghold over the area. A wall was needed to keep the barbarians out.

Employing the labor of convicts, conscripted citizens, and soldiers, Meng joined together the remnants of walls that had been built by earlier Chinese states to create one massive wall. The wall was said to extend more than 10,000 *li,* with one *li* approximately .3 miles (.5 km). While no one measured the exact length of the wall at the time, the number *10,000* was Chinese shorthand for "really long" in much the same way that the word *gazillion* is used today to indicate enormity. This was the beginning of what has come to be known as the Great Wall of China.

In addition to the Great Wall and the canal, Meng also supervised the creation of the Straight Road, which ran some 500 miles (805 km) northward to the Ordos region. The road was intended to facilitate the military and colonial conquest of the Ordos. Public works projects on such a massive scale could be undertaken only by an empire that could command the labor of millions of people beholden to the emperor.

Qin Shi Huangdi's public works projects were not limited to those with public and military benefit, however. Obsessed with a desire to find the secrets of immortality, in 212 BCE the emperor ordered the construction of his own tomb, an enormous underground building populated by an army of seven thousand life-size terra-cotta clay soldiers. He also ordered expeditions to islands said to be populated by immortals in hopes of finding elixirs that could prolong his life. Despite his efforts, he died on just such an expedition in 210 BCE.

When Qin Shi Huangdi's son was crowned as the second emperor, discontent arose throughout the empire. The second emperor had been on the throne only a year when a series of revolts, led by poor farmers, resulted in the overthrow of the regime and the beginning of a new order: the Han Dynasty.

The Han Dynasty Comes to Power

The new ruler of the Han Dynasty, Gaozu, had risen up from poverty and therefore had great compassion for the poor. He became a symbol of hope for millions of Chinese who also sought to rise from poverty.

As the new ruler, Gaozu ruled directly over the area to the north and west of the capital. To the south and east, however, he gave limited control of the region to ten kingdoms, whose leaders vowed to support his empire. Over time he replaced the leaders of these kingdoms with military leaders and officials loyal to him. He gave them official titles and the ability to raise taxes, part of which were paid to the emperor and some of which could be kept for their own personal use.

Gaozu focused on creating a stable political system in China by reinforcing the bureaucracy created by the Qin. He created ranks of administrators. These included three excellencies who were in charge of different aspects of the government, supported by nine ministers, each with different, overlapping responsibilities to ensure that no single person gained too much power.

Gaozu was a down-to-earth leader who bragged that he had won his empire on horseback as a soldier. Since he had no experience running a government, he needed to recruit civil servants to oversee the empire and adopted Confucian values to guide his government. For the next few centuries, the Han bureaucracy and civil service was run by scholars educated in Confucian values and recruited to serve the government. Eligible scholars from an imperial academy took a civil service examination each year, based largely on their studies of Confucian texts. A corps of bureaucrats was chosen to run the government based on the results of this exam. The testing system allowed individuals on the bottom of the social ladder to rise to the top through hard work and study. A new class of scholar-officials grew into a powerful political force in the subsequent centuries of Chinese history.

The Wrath of an Emperor

In his zeal to create a new society, Qin Shi Huangdi was not always respectful of what had come before, particularly in the way of scholarship. In 213 BCE the emperor became angry that scholars had cited historical records in criticizing him for abandoning feudalism. In response, according to Han historian Sima Qian, who wrote a century later, the emperor ordered that 460 Confucian scholars be buried alive. He also ordered scholars to turn over all historical records to be burned. Copies of Confucian works in particular were collected and burned by the hundreds. Surviving the literary holocaust were books on technical subjects such as agriculture, which the emperor and his legalist advisers determined were too important to burn.

Gaozu instituted two other routes to employment in the government. One of these, called search and recommend, encouraged government officials to nominate upright citizens to serve in the government as civil servants. Another path to government jobs revolved around recruitment of filial citizens. Filial piety, or devotion to parents and superiors, was one of the most important Confucian doctrines. It included an awareness of one's place in society and respect for elders and those of higher rank. According to historian Patricia Buckley Ebrey, the following Confucian text on filial piety was used during the Han Dynasty to teach children Confucian values while they learned to read:

The Master [Confucius] said, "Filial piety is the root of virtue and the source of civilization. Since we receive our body, hair, and skin from our parents, we do not dare let it be injured in any way. This is the beginning of filial piety. We establish ourselves and practice the Way [of Confucianism], thereby perpetuating our name for future generations and bringing glory to parents. This is the fulfillment of filial piety. Thus, filial piety begins with serving our parents, continues with serving the ruler, and is completed by establishing one's character."[13]

The Benefits of a Stable Political System

The Han Dynasty, which lasted from 206 BCE to 220 CE, was one of the most enduring dynasties in Chinese history. Stability brought peace, and the two together created opportunities for experimentation with new ideas and inventions. One of these inventions was paper. The availability of paper resulted in the growth of literacy beyond the very highest classes and allowed a culture of scholarship to take root at all levels of society.

Improvements in scholarship were also made possible by a vast improvement in nutrition and health that resulted from two new inventions: pig iron and the blast furnace. Pig iron was a crude form of iron created by smelting ore at high heat using blast furnaces, which blasted superheated air to extract metal from ore. From iron, Chinese craftsmen created farming tools such as the iron plow, which enabled

Scholars in ancient China take the civil service exam that will determine who obtains powerful government positions. A new class of scholar-officials emerged from this system of testing.

farmers to break up soil, sow seeds, and harvest an abundance of crops. As agriculture grew and changed, nutrition and health improved, the population expanded, and scholars began to make academic leaps. The scholarship of the Han era, for example, led to a number of mathematical discoveries, among them, negative numbers.

The Challenge of the Northern Frontier

While the Han Dynasty ruled during a period of relative peace and stability, the era was not without challenges—particularly along the northern border. During the Qin Dynasty, Xiongnu raids in the Ordos region had led to the building of stronger and longer walls. The Han emperor continued this practice but also began to experiment with a very different policy toward the Xiongnu: harmonious kinship.

Harmonious kinship was an attempt to engage the Xiongnu as friends. Around 200 BCE a Chinese princess was sent to the Xiongnu leader as a bride in the hopes of cementing a bond of marriage between the two cultures. Han leaders also sent a yearly tribute of gifts—silk and grains—items the Xiongnu could not obtain except through trade or pillaging. Lastly, the Han emperor acknowledged the worth of both peoples by recognizing a new border delineating Xiongnu territory and Chinese territory. While this policy worked for a time, later Han rulers tried again to resolve the Xiongnu problem with military might. From 133 to 119 BCE the Han emperor sent between one hundred thousand and three hundred thousand soldiers to fight the Xiongnu under two powerful generals. These generals secured victory—for a time.

Developing Trade

Despite the Han's struggles, the empire's attempts to secure allies in its fight with the Xiongnu led to expanding trade in other parts of Asia and the beginning of the Silk Road trade route. In 138 BCE Zhang Qian, a civilian official in the Han Dynasty, went on an expedition seeking military allies. After being captured and detained by the Xiongnu for ten years, Zhang was set free and journeyed west to central Asia. There he not only continued a diplomatic mission but also established a trade mission on behalf of the Han. When he finally returned to the Han court, he reported on the regions, countries, and products available for trading partnerships. These included horses from Fergana (in modern-day Uzbekistan), alfalfa from central Asia, grapes and precious stones from Persia, and wools from herds throughout Asia and the Middle East. All of this could be traded for Han silk, which was well known by 200 BCE for its beauty and elegance.

Despite the Han Dynasty's strides in expanding foreign trade and appeasing the people of the north, in the final century the edges of the empire began to fray. Smaller kingdoms within the empire began splintering off and struggling among themselves. By the third century CE, the Han Dynasty was falling apart.

Chapter 3

The Rise of the Northern Dynasties

China's relationship with the people of the northern regions fluctuated over hundreds of years between periods of conflict and periods of peace. Stark differences between north and south brought animosity and mistrust, as well as a sharing of knowledge, ideas, and traditions.

The people of the Han cradle, in the south, built a civilization that revolved around agriculture. With rich soil, abundant food, and plentiful water, the inhabitants had the time, space, and resources to develop other pursuits, including pottery and metalwork, literacy, and music.

The people of the harsh northern steppes were pastoralists, animal-herders who built a nomadic civilization. They traveled from place to place, carrying few possessions. Their lives revolved around their animals. Their herds of sheep and camels provided meat and milk, wool and leather, and fuel for fires. Unlike their southern neighbors, they did not have the time, space, or resources to develop literacy, or the types of art and music common in Confucian cultures.

The differences between the northern and southern peoples did not entirely prevent a mixing of cultures. Cultural exchanges occurred voluntarily at times but more often it took place when the peoples of the north swooped down on and conquered portions of the south or when the farmers of the south pressed north to carve out more agricultural lands. The northern dynasties, for as long as they lasted, left their mark on Chinese life and culture.

The Cultural Adaptation of the Northern Wei Dynasty

The Northern Wei Dynasty, which ruled China from 386 to 535 CE had its roots among the Tuoba people of Mongolia. The Tuoba's territory lay at the border between China's agricultural areas and the dry steppes. Living in this transitional zone, the Tuoba were able to gain control of primary invasion routes into northern China, overcoming other ethnic groups in the region. The Tuoba's horsemanship and military prowess enabled them to conquer and unify much of the north, annexing five states between 431 and 440.

In 386 the Tuoba adopted the ancient name of Wei and established the Northern Wei Dynasty with a capital in what is now Shanxi Province. At first the Wei warriors had little patience for the agricultural people they conquered. The warriors looked down on the sedentary population. They restricted the movements of the population and prohibited marriage outside their ethnic group.

In conquering an agricultural population, however, the Wei ran into a problem that would plague northern rulers for centuries. They discovered that it was easier to conquer an agricultural people than to govern them. Wei leaders looked to Chinese administrators and bureaucrats for help in levying taxes and running government institutions. Chinese advisers introduced the Wei Dynasty to administrative structures as well as the Chinese penal code. Over time the Wei ruling class began taking on more and more Chinese ways and losing their own pastoral traditions. Historians call this process of becoming Chinese *Sinicization*. According to historian Jacques Gernet, the process of Sinicization happened over the course of centuries:

> The gradual conversion to a sedentary existence, the decline in the importance of the horse as a result of the role played by infantry in the wars against the Yangtze empires, and the growing importance of revenues with an agricultural origin (cereals and cloth) gradually changed the empire's economy. Finally, the attraction of the products of Chinese craftsmen, the taste

Han Dynasty artisans create objects from clay. Thanks to abundant food and water, the people of the Han civilization had time to develop other pursuits, including the art of making pottery.

for luxury, the prestige of Chinese culture, and the preponderant influence of Buddhism transformed the mentality of the Tuoba aristocracy.[14]

Wei leaders adopted many of the philosophical beliefs of the Chinese dynasties, such as a legalist philosophy and bureaucracy. The state had tight control over the population. Peasants were organized in much the same way they had been during the Qin Dynasty. Five families formed a neighborhood, or *lin*. Five *lin* formed a village, or *li*. And five *li* formed a commune, or *tang*. Each *tang* was charged with the task of cultivating as much land as possible. Leaders at each level were appointed by the government.

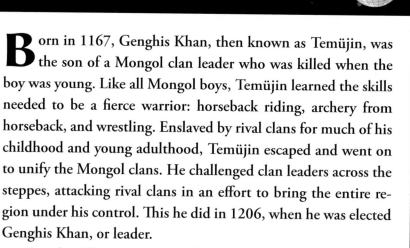

Genghis Khan

Born in 1167, Genghis Khan, then known as Temüjin, was the son of a Mongol clan leader who was killed when the boy was young. Like all Mongol boys, Temüjin learned the skills needed to be a fierce warrior: horseback riding, archery from horseback, and wrestling. Enslaved by rival clans for much of his childhood and young adulthood, Temüjin escaped and went on to unify the Mongol clans. He challenged clan leaders across the steppes, attacking rival clans in an effort to bring the entire region under his control. This he did in 1206, when he was elected Genghis Khan, or leader.

Genghis Khan was a popular leader among the Mongols, who viewed his rule as both fair and brutal. He created a code of law—a strict moral code—for the Mongols, including loyalty to himself. Harsh penalties, including death, were the consequence of violations such as lying, black magic, and theft.

Genghis Khan sought to conquer as much of the known world as possible. He is said to have told his men that a man's chief joy and goal in life is to "conquer one's enemies, to pursue them, to deprive them of their possessions, to reduce their families to tears."

Quoted in *The Mongolian Conquests: Time Frame 1200–1300 AD.* Alexandria, VA: Time-Life Books, 1989, p.13.

Wei rulers even went so far as to spread agriculture into the north as a way to provide a larger buffer zone between nomadic groups and the broader Chinese populace. If the land was cultivated, it was no longer suitable for grazing, and the wild horsemen would be pushed further north. The Wei government deported hundreds of thousands of people to live in and cultivate arid regions. From 386 to 409, during the reign of Tao Wu Ti, 460,000 people were relocated to the north. By the late 400s the Northern Wei had transformed from a nomadic, pastoral group into a sedentary, agricultural dynasty. To complete the transformation, it moved its capital south to the agricultural region of Luoyang.

The integration of cultures could be seen in many aspects of daily life. The ruling family took a Chinese name and insisted that others wear Chinese clothes, use Chinese names, and practice Chinese manners. They also insisted that others convert to Buddhism, the religion adopted by the aristocracy. As historian Su Shuyang notes,

> In the north, particularly, the assimilation of the Han and non-Han ethnic groups continued for almost 150 years. The merging of these ethnic groups was reflected in the cultural relics of the time. . . . It is unquestionable that many Han surnames originated with non-Han people. This kind of open exchange greatly aided the development of Chinese civilization.[15]

Not everyone was happy about the Wei Dynasty's Sinicization. The army and lower classes, living on the outskirts of society to protect borders, still followed nomadic traditions. As the capital moved south, the military received less respect than ever before. This led to resentment and eventually rebellion by military factions still skilled in the warfare techniques of the steppes. Rebellion led to civil war and ultimately the end of the Wei Dynasty around 535.

Mixing Cultures

During some periods, northern and southern ethnic groups mixed through intermarriage. Some dynasties sent gifts in exchange for peace.

One such dynasty was the Sui Dynasty (581–618), first ruled by Emperor Wendi. Wendi tried to unify China by making trade and cultural exchange easier and by setting an example of the mixing of cultures himself. His court played host to many intermarriages between northern rulers and Chinese aristocrats.

One of Wendi's lasting contributions was the reform of legal and tax codes, synthesizing northern and southern practices into a form that would be emulated throughout Chinese history. According to historian J.A.G. Roberts, this Kaihuang Code "defined crimes and their punishments in plain terms and allowed guilty officials to commute their punishment by payments of a fine or by accepting demotion. The Kaihuang Code was to provide a model for all future imperial legal codes."[16]

But although Wendi encouraged intermarriages and the mixing of cultures to unify China, he also sought to protect the nation from northern aggression. Utilizing the forced labor of peasants, he repaired the Great Wall and amassed a vast army to protect the border. He established farming communities in the border regions by forcing families to move north and by building a canal and a fleet of boats to move rice and other products from the south into the north. Wendi did not live to see the canal's completion. That task fell to his second son, Emperor Yangdi. According to Roberts, Yangdi vastly expanded on his father's initial idea, creating a whole complex of waterways:

> Yangdi carried [canal building] much further, creating a network of canals extending about 1200 miles [1,931 km], which has been described as "probably an engineering feat without parallel in the world of its time." This national system of communications was to provide the basis for the prosperity for later dynasties.[17]

These canals, which came to be known as the Grand Canal system, connected northern and southern China in a way they had not been linked before. Because China's main rivers run west to east, it had been easier to connect the eastern and western parts of the region. The canal changed the geographic equation by making it easier for people, goods, communications, and ideas to travel between north and south.

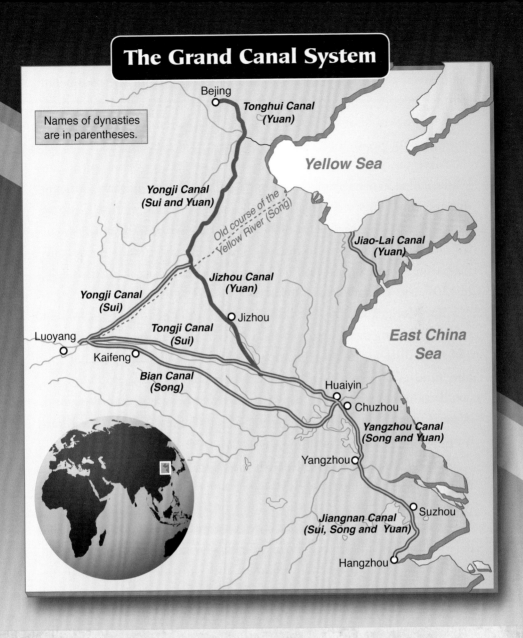

The Grand Canal System

Names of dynasties are in parentheses.

Bejing

Tonghui Canal (Yuan)

Yellow Sea

Yongji Canal (Sui and Yuan)

Old course of the Yellow River (Song)

Jiao-Lai Canal (Yuan)

Jizhou Canal (Yuan)

Yongji Canal (Sui)

Jizhou

Tongji Canal (Sui)

Luoyang

Kaifeng

Bian Canal (Song)

East China Sea

Huaiyin

Chuzhou

Yangzhou Canal (Song and Yuan)

Yangzhou

Suzhou

Jiangnan Canal (Sui, Song and Yuan)

Hangzhou

Ultimately reaching from Hangzhou to Beijing, the canal became China's premiere trade route.

Mongol Rule

Not every dynasty sought to mix northern and southern cultures. Unlike the Wei Dynasty, which adopted Chinese ways, the Yuan Dynasty, established by the Mongols who came from what is now Mongolia, maintained a sense of superiority and separation from the conquered Chinese people. From the perspective of the Mongols and their leaders, China represented only one part of a much larger empire, one conquest among many begun long before the dynasty was established.

After unifying the Mongols in the late 1100s, Temüjin, a clan leader, called a meeting of all Mongol nobility, known as khans. During that meeting, which took place in 1206, the group elected him Genghis Khan, which meant Emperor of All Men, and gave him the power to set the course of Mongol conquest. He set his sights on lands far beyond his borders—to China—and built up an enormous army. At its height in 1207, the Mongol army numbered a quarter million.

The Mongol military was divided into units of highly disciplined soldiers working on campaigns that varied from short term to long term and short distance to long distance. In subdivided fighting units of ten, one hundred, one thousand, and ten thousand soldiers, the Mongols could coordinate troop movements with swiftness and precision. And because every unit leader had personal connections to Genghis Khan himself, the Mongol leader had the army under tight control.

Mongol tacticians demonstrated superiority in warfare. As skilled horsemen, the Mongols could quickly move into regions difficult to reach for foot soldiers or chariots. Additionally, Genghis Khan had perfected some key military tricks. The Mongols were famous for withdrawing from a battle scene during the heaviest fighting, signaling their own defeat. Pursued by their enemies, the Mongols would lead them to a trap in which a cavalry of armored soldiers would descend to devastate the enemy army.

Mongol warfare was a family affair. Genghis Khan's sons were given responsibility for different territories and campaigns east into Europe, south into Persia, southwest into Afghanistan, and south into China. Upon his death, Genghis Khan's empire fell apart, divided among three sons and a grandson. His son, Ögödei, campaigned against the Chinese at their northern border, pushing south down the Yellow River into Sichuan.

The farther south they pushed, the more resistance the Mongols met among the Chinese. Throughout the thirteenth century, Chinese military resistance, walls, and the wet terrain of the south hindered Mongol success. It was hard for a cavalry to fight in the swampy fields of rice farmers. The horsemen could not easily sweep across plains when confronted with miles of thick mud. It was not until grandson Kublai Khan took control of the campaign that all of China truly came under Mongol rule.

Kublai Khan's "First Beginning"

From the very beginning of his rule, Kublai Khan looked to the Chinese for ways to build China into a strong power. In 1260 he moved his capital south to what is now Beijing to better oversee the region, and he began rebuilding the city that had been destroyed by his grandfather nearly forty years before. In 1271 Kublai Khan declared himself emperor of a new dynasty, Da Yuan, translated as "Great Origin" or "First Beginning."

By 1279 Kublai Khan's armies had finally overcome the last rebels from the previous dynasty. At last he could focus on ruling rather than fighting. But Kublai Khan recognized that the Mongols were inexperienced in running a bureaucracy and at living a sedentary, agricultural life. He listened to a close adviser, a Buddhist monk, who said, "One can conquer the world on horseback; one cannot govern it on horseback."[18] To govern, Kublai Khan sought the advice of Chinese administrators but often hired foreigners instead. According to historian Bamber Gascoigne,

> From the start, Kublai had shown his intention of governing along Chinese lines. Even when his rule extended no further than a fief given him by his brother in the Wei valley, he had set up at Xian a traditional Chinese system of administration. But there was one crucial respect in which he had to depart from the normal pattern. For obvious reasons, as a rank and much resented intruder, he preferred the Chinese civil service to Chinese civil servants. A few carefully selected scholars were invited to hold office, but the examinations were suspended and

were not resumed until 1315, when they were given a built-in bias against Chinese candidates. On the other hand, there were not enough Mongols with the ability to fill the higher ranks in the administration. Kublai's solution was to employ foreigners, a considerable supply of whom had been made available by the new stability of Central Asia.[19]

An Open-Minded Ruler

Kublai Khan and his dynasty were open-minded and cosmopolitan. They sought and employed people of all nationalities and philosophies to run and advise the government, including Italian explorer and merchant Marco Polo. An Arab architect was commissioned to rebuild Beijing and create palaces and parks. Foreign soldiers were hired to work in the Mongol army as well.

The Mongols' openness was also evident in their dealings with religion. Kublai Khan's mother had been a Nestorian Christian, a faith that had come to Mongolia from Constantinople. Kublai Khan himself, however, practiced a mixture of Buddhism and animism, a belief that spirits exist within ordinary objects and animals. He was open to the many religions practiced by the people of China and the newly conquered regions, including Daoism, Confucianism, Buddhism, Islam, and Nestorian Christianity.

The one group to which Kublai Khan was less open was the Chinese themselves. The complex social hierarchy within the Yuan court put Mongols at the top, followed by foreigners such as Persians, Russians, and central Asian Muslims. Third in importance were the northern Chinese. At the bottom of society were southern Chinese. In an effort to recruit a greater diversity of people—and keep Chinese scholars out of power—Kublai Khan stopped the tradition of using scores on Confucian civil service exams to determine who was qualified to serve in the government. He opened the civil service up to non-Chinese scholars from many provinces and regions.

Mongol openness to foreign influences led to an increase in foreign trade under the Yuan Dynasty. Now that the Silk Road was under one

Marco Polo Describes Kublai Khan's China

Much of what is known about the court of Kublai Khan comes from the writings of Marco Polo, a merchant from Venice who traveled to China and stayed to become a part of Kublai Khan's retinue for seventeen years. He described Kublai Khan's palace as "the greatest and most wonderful that was ever seen." He told of mansions with four hundred rooms and chambers so large that six thousand people could dine at the same time. He described a garden created on a man-made pile of dirt 328 feet (100 m) high, crowned by a beautiful pavilion and covered with trees taken from different parts of China. He wrote, "Whenever his majesty receives information of a handsome tree growing in any place, he causes it to be dug up, with all its roots and earth about them, and . . . transported by means of elephants to this mount."

Quoted in Jonathan Fryer, *The Great Wall of China*. London: New English Library, 1975, p. 116.

Quoted in Nicholas C.J. Pappas, "The Travels of Marco Polo," Sam Houston University. www .shsu.edu.

rule from one end to the other, merchants could travel the whole length in relative safety, and exotic goods began to travel from Constantinople to China and back. Francesco Balducci Pegalotti, a merchant traveling on the road around 1340, wrote pages of practical notes about how to set about on a Silk Road journey. Among his writings are lists of products available to buyers all along the route. These included "Slavonian squirrels, martins and finches, goat skins and ram skins, dates, filberts, walnuts, salted sturgeon tails . . . round pepper, ginger . . . raw silk, saffron, clove-stalks and cloves, nutmegs, spike, cardamoms . . . dragon's blood, sweetmeats, gold wire, dressed silk and much else besides."[20]

Muslims from central Asia were important to keeping trade flowing along the Silk Road. They imported such goods as jewels, carpets, spices, and even camels, and they carried away luxury items such as silk, porcelain, and lacquerware. Muslims served the Mongol court as architects, doctors, astronomers, and as artists, such as poets and musicians. They also served in a role repugnant to the Chinese populace: tax collectors.

Hardship Under the Yuan Dynasty

Historians differ on whether the Yuan Dynasty helped or hurt China's poor. High taxes, paid in the form of crops, took as much as 70 percent of crops away from the countryside, leading to widespread hunger. In addition, the brutality of the Mongols' ongoing military campaigns and the starvation and disease that followed war led to a sharp decline in population. Also, visiting traders and armies may have brought the plague to China. Between the thirteenth and fourteenth centuries, due to plague, wars, and famine, the population of China fell from 100 million people to between 60 and 80 million.

In addition to a drop in population, ethnic Chinese suffered in other ways, too. For all his openness to foreign workers and goods, Kublai Khan took an opposite approach when it came to the Han Chinese. Ethnic Chinese people lived under many restrictions. For example, they were forbidden from owning or carrying arms, including bamboo, which could be used to make bows and arrows. Chinese and Mongol people were forbidden to intermarry. And each maintained its view of the other culture as barbaric or weak.

The Legacy of the Yuan Dynasty

The Yuan Dynasty was a mixed blessing for the people of China. Despite wars, famine, and plague, many historians believe Mongol rule had a positive effect on Chinese society. Although taxes were high at first, the Mongols later focused on tax relief for the peasantry. They increased agricultural production, maintained water systems to prevent floods, created a postal system, took care of the poor, and created granaries to

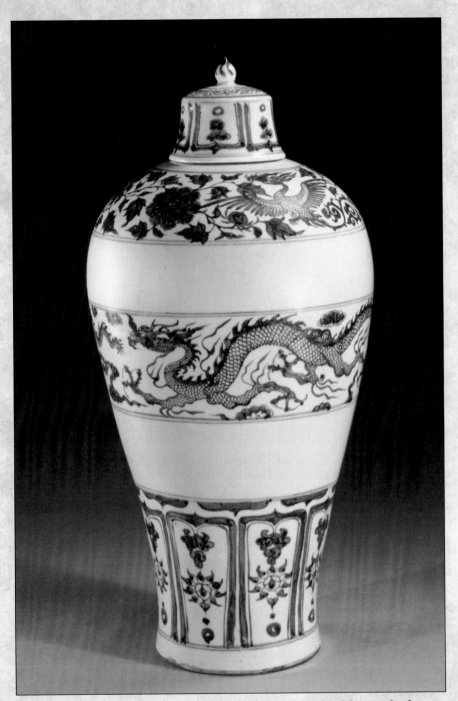

A dragon, a phoenix, clouds, and flowers decorate this blue and white
porcelain vase from the Yuan Dynasty of the Mongol era. Artistic
endeavor reached new heights during this period.

store surplus grains in case of famine. Yet while the Mongols supported peasants in many ways, they continued to exploit the poor through forced labor on public works projects. From the extension of the Grand Canal to the postal station system, to the reconstruction of what is now Beijing, peasants provided unpaid, forced labor. This caused great resentment among the peasantry.

While peasants enjoyed the mixed blessing of Mongol rule, artists and craftsmen gained a new celebrity status. According to the Columbia University website Asia for Educators:

> The benefits artisans gained from Mongol rule include freedom from corvée (unpaid) labor, tax remissions, and higher social status. Thus, artisanship reached new heights in the Mongol era. Spectacular textiles and porcelains were produced, and blue and white porcelains, a style generally associated with the Ming dynasty, were actually first developed during the Mongol era.[21]

In addition, with so many scholars and civil servants unemployed by the government, many took to writing. The epic dramas of the period, featuring the clash between Confucian ideals and human passion, became the basis of many classical Chinese plays.

The high costs of building so many public structures, and the high taxes assessed to pay for those projects, led to the collapse of the Yuan Dynasty. The taxes could not begin to pay for the maintenance of the Grand Canal and other water systems. In the 1340s devastating floods swept through the land, leaving many people homeless. These homeless peasants banded together into rebel groups that grew in number and power, ultimately enabling them to bring down the Mongol rulers.

Chapter 4

The Golden Ages of Dynastic Rule

A golden age is a period in the life of a country in which the economy grows; arts, culture, and scholarship flourish; and ordinary people thrive. Generally, golden ages are periods of peace and community following times of war and disunity. Many historians believe that China experienced golden ages during several dynasties, particularly the Tang Dynasty (618–907), the Song Dynasty (960–1279), and the Ming Dynasty (1368–1644). Each of these dynasties left a lasting legacy that influenced Chinese history and culture for years to come.

The Tang Dynasty

Historian J.A.G. Roberts considered the Tang Dynasty to be one of these golden ages, particularly under the rule of the second Tang emperor, Taizong. Roberts writes, "Taizong has been regarded by Confucianists as a model ruler, a view echoed in the West where he has been described as 'probably the greatest monarch in China's history.'"[22] For the first ten years of his reign, from 626 through 636, Taizong focused on creating a dynamic system of civil service to run China. He employed able advisers who modeled, according to Roberts, the ideal relationship between monarch and councillor. Instead of always telling the emperor what he wanted to hear, they gave him their honest opinions and their best advice.

As a result, Taizong's bureaucracy was well run and well organized. The country was divided into governmental regions, much like states, counties, and cities. The largest of these regions were called circuits and were administered by commissioners. Circuits were divided into prefectures governed by prefects and again subdivided into districts ruled by magistrates. Each had a built-in system of checks and balances to prevent misuse of power. A secretariat wrote laws, a chancellery checked the laws, a state department carried out laws, a censorate investigated abuses of power, and a supreme court conducted trials and reviews of the laws.

Although the Tang Dynasty had its roots in the intermarriage between Chinese and non-Chinese people, Tang rulers still struggled to manage relations with the north. When Turks invaded China early in his reign, Taizong allied with northerners to defeat the invaders. Later Tang rulers used marriage as a tool of diplomacy, sending Chinese princesses north to marry leaders of the steppe peoples in an attempt to cement relations. In a departure from previous dynasties, the Tang also experimented with indirect rule. This allowed members of some groups to govern themselves while overall control firmly remained with the Tang. The Yue ethnic group, for example, was incorporated into the Tang system of government with some measure of independence. Traditional tribal leaders were recruited to government positions, allowing them to govern their own people on behalf of the Tang.

Art and Artists Thrive

The Tang period is perhaps best known for an explosion of creativity in the arts. Some of China's most famous poets lived and wrote during the Tang. According to historian Roberts, "The poetry written during that reign was later regarded as a model which all Chinese poets might try to emulate, but could never hope to surpass. An eighteenth-century anthology, the *Three Hundred Tang Poems,* has become a treasure of poems familiar to all educated Chinese."[23]

Tang poets and artists were often concerned with humankind's connection with nature. Poems such as the following verse by one of China's most famous poets, Wang Wei (699–759) celebrated a simple life in the outdoors. This poem refers to a tradition of offering the gift of a willow bow to a departing traveler:

Willow Waves
The two rows of perfect trees
Fall reflected in the clear ripples
And do not copy those by the palace moat
Where the spring wind sharpens the goodbye.[24]

The visual arts also celebrated nature. Painters divided into two clear schools, now called the northern Tang and southern Tang schools. Painters of the southern school tended to be amateurs who painted landscapes of monochromatic brushwork. Painters of the northern school were often court painters and professionals who used vivid colors to create ornate scenes involving people. Horses played a prominent role in Tang art as well because horses played an important role in Tang culture. The Tang restored China's cavalry, increasing the number of horses from 5,000 to 706,000 in fifty years, and this change is evident in the number of horses appearing in Tang paintings.

Horses are a common theme in Tang Dynasty artwork, as can be seen in this Tang-era depiction of horses and riders. Horses played a prominent role in both the art and culture of the period.

When the Tang Dynasty finally fell from power, a period of chaos ensued, with five dynasties ruling China in fifty years. That period lasted from 907 to 960. Out of this chaos arose another of the golden age dynasties: the Song Dynasty.

The Rise of the Song Dynasty

The first Song emperor came to power as a result of a coup against the short-lived later Zhou Dynasty in 960. The coup leader, a general named Zhao, and a group of military commanders wrested control of the government from the hands of an infant emperor and a distrusted dowager empress. Zhao agreed to become emperor only after military leaders pledged unconditional obedience to him. As emperor, he took the name Taizu. He reigned as the first emperor of the Song Dynasty, a dynasty that lasted until 1279 CE.

Taizu began his rule with a series of rapid and wise decisions that would determine the course and tone of the dynasty for its duration. Upon entering the capital, Bianjing, for the first time, Taizu issued a decree forbidding his troops from plundering the city or harming civilians. He insisted that the imperial family not be killed and instead be allowed to exit office and live peacefully. These decrees showed a radically different orientation from that of most emperors, who were quick to loot, plunder, and kill their enemies. To prevent continued military uprisings, he held a banquet for the generals and persuaded them to retire with generous pensions far away from the city. With these diplomatic moves, Taizu ensured a peaceful start to what would become a golden age of stability and enlightenment in China's dynamic dynastic history.

A Government Run by Scholars

From the start the Song Dynasty was different from those that came before it. While Taizu sought to unify China, he did so with leniency and intelligence. He recruited the best minds in China to run the government. To do so, he broke with long-standing traditions that allowed wealthy ruling families easy access to administrative jobs.

The Beginning of Standardized Tests

Standardized tests were an important factor in selecting civil servants in many Chinese dynasties. The Song Dynasty examinations, which determined whether a scholar could enter public service as a government adviser or administrator, were among the most rigorous and intense the world has ever seen. Scholars often spent a lifetime preparing for exams. Only top scorers were recommended for government service.

On exam days, test takers arrived at dawn. They brought enough food to last for the duration of the test, which could be hours or days. Test takers sat in tiny private kiosks that were locked and sometimes marked with a seal to prevent anyone from entering or exiting during the exam. The Chinese had always been concerned with cheating. In the Han Dynasty, leaders tried to keep cheaters from knowing test questions by having each candidate shoot through a list of questions with a bow and arrow. The questions their arrow pierced were the questions they would have to answer.

Bias was also a concern. Tang Dynasty examiners tried to prevent bias by covering the candidate's name on the examination paper before it was graded. Under the Song Dynasty, exam answers were recopied by a government worker so no one could recognize the test taker's handwriting.

For centuries wealthy and well-connected families had managed to place their sons into positions of power, regardless of how they fared on the civil service exams. Whereas military service was a way of rising in social class in many dynasties, scholarship soon also became a means of improving oneself, even for those of lowly birth. Those who scored highest on state tests were to lead China. Taizu and his brother,

Taizong, who advised him and succeeded him on the throne, explained their reasoning to an angry aristocracy: "We are concerned that bosoms clothed in coarse fabrics may carry qualities of jade, and the fact remain unknown."[25] In other words, brilliant minds may be found in the poorest peasants, and examinations were a way of discovering these bright new administrators.

The Blossoming of the Arts

In addition to transforming government, the Song Dynasty's emphasis on scholarship had another effect: a blossoming of the arts. The ideal government official was both an artist and an intellectual—a scholarartist. Taizong, an avid calligrapher, commissioned the creation of artistic and scholarly works, such as encyclopedias, and gathered the work of centuries in art collections and catalogs that still exist today.

Cities grew in size and importance during this period, reaching populations of fifty thousand before the end of the Song Dynasty. Although dynastic leaders lived in cities, they valued country life. As in the Tang Dynasty, much of the art produced during the Song celebrated the human relationship with nature. Spontaneity was also highly valued. Taking up brushes and black ink, an artist might not be sure if what would appear on paper would be a poem written in Chinese characters or a "wordless poem" in the form of a picture. Buddhist monks became some of the cultural leaders in this style of painting.

The eighth Song emperor, Huizong, invited scholar-artists to participate in poetry-art competitions. He presented competitors with a line or two of poetry—written in beautiful calligraphy—and then asked them to spontaneously create a painting based on the verse. On one occasion he assigned the following line: "The horses hooves were fragrant on returning from trampling flowers."[26] The winner of that competition painted airy butterflies fluttering around heavy horse hooves.

Song Dynasty arts were not limited to brush painting and poetry. Pottery had long been an important industry in China. Copper and bronze were used to make bowls and vessels for household use. Just before the dynasty began, however, a copper shortage sent artists

During the Song Dynasty, artisans developed a light green glaze that came to be known, along with the pottery it covered, as celadon. Celadon was one of the many prized objects traded by merchants traveling along the Silk Road.

scrambling for other ways to create their works of usable art. New glazes were developed, including a distinctive cobalt blue and white glaze for porcelain. During the Song Dynasty, glazed porcelain objects and stoneware bathed in a greenish glaze (both the pottery and glaze came to be known as celadon) achieved purity and beauty not seen before this time. These were valued commodities on the developing Silk Road trade route between China and the West. Traders brought goods from the Near East to China and spread China's luxury items—silk, porcelain, and stoneware—as far away as Africa.

Printing and Inventions

The Song celebration of intellectual pursuits went hand in hand with the development of printing and other technologies. While paper had been invented by the Chinese around the first century CE, the ability to print came much later. During the Song Dynasty printing technology developed rapidly. Woodblocks were used for the first time to print the same text more than once. This led to the creation of extensive libraries. From 981 onward, the Song Dynasty published encyclopedias of the collected writings of centuries and volumes of works on architecture, medicine, botany, and zoology. A *Compendium of Military Technology*, published about 1080, gave instructions for making gunpowder for use in fireworks, fireballs, and bombs. And the *Comprehensive Mirror for Aid in Government*, published around 1084, described the flow of Chinese history from ancient times to the Song. Perhaps most important to the people of China was the printing of the entire works of Confucius as well as Daoist and Buddhist religious texts. Renzong, a later Song emperor, was said to have a library containing more than eighty thousand volumes of scholarly studies.

Important inventions were also created during the Song Dynasty. The blossoming of scholarship, curiosity, and study led to the development of such world-changing inventions as the magnetic compass, the abacus, topographical relief maps, and one of the first complex mechanical clocks.

Neglect Leads to Downfall

Song emperors were so focused on intellectual pursuits that they neglected military preparedness and economic growth, particularly in managing the northern border. In the first decades of Song rule, 375,000 soldiers were stationed along the northern border. By 1045, that number had tripled to 1.25 million. Though this represented a huge buildup, the vast majority of soldiers were poorly paid and poorly trained.

Troops on the border were not adequately prepared to protect China from the Liao and the Jin, the two most aggressive tribes of the north. Knowing this, the government sought to appease them by offering a yearly tribute. The problem, however, was that the price of tribute increased each year. Peace could be neither forced nor bought from the tribes of the north.

As government coffers dwindled, the Song Dynasty began to look toward the countryside for more revenue. Taxes increased for the peasantry but not for the increasingly privileged scholar class. The Song Dynasty began to unravel as attacks from the north and unrest in the countryside caused massive upheaval. China would have to wait hundreds of years before a new golden age graced the pages of its history.

The Ming Dynasty

That new golden age began with the Ming Dynasty, around 1368. Many of China's most recognizable monuments were built during the Ming era. But for all its accomplishments, the Ming Dynasty had humble beginnings, springing out of the hardship and deprivation of the Yuan Dynasty that came before it. The first Ming emperor, Hongwu, had seen firsthand the devastating effects of Mongol rule on the Chinese countryside. His first order of business was to restore agriculture to its former place as the center of the Chinese economy. He paid for the relocation of peasants to land that had previously been more pastoral than agricultural. Their job was to farm the land. To ensure an adequate supply for irrigating crops, Hongwu had dikes and canals restored and new reservoirs built. Forty-one thousand reservoirs were created or fixed in 1395. Within eight years his investment in agriculture and water systems had tripled in profits. With a restored water system, the Ming Dynasty was able to keep produce and products moving throughout China's extensive canal system.

To heal a deforested countryside and provide wood for a new shipbuilding industry, Hongwu had 50 million trees planted around Nanjing in 1391. Each family settling on colonized land was given 200 mulberry, jujube, and persimmon trees to plant. In all, it is thought that a billion trees were planted under Hongwu's command.

Hongwu's strong leadership breathed new life into China's farming and food production. The same forcefulness he brought to that task shaped his overall style of governance. Hongwu valued power, and he did not hesitate to use it. As emperor, he abandoned the system of checks and balances that had existed in earlier dynasties, opting instead for consolidation of power under his own personal control. While he publicly advocated for Confucian restraint and respect, he displayed his power in a most un-Confucian way by treating lesser officials in his government harshly and subjecting them to unpredictable punishments and public beatings.

Hongwu divided up governance of the empire by giving control of provincial regions to many of his thirty-six sons. Each was given total authority to govern his region, and those near the border were responsible for defense. Upon his death in 1398, several of Hongwu's sons and grandsons fought for control of the dynasty. In the end, Yongle, whose name meant "Perpetual Happiness," came to power.

Ming Monuments and Accomplishments

Yongle ruled from 1402 to 1424. He was responsible for creating many of China's most famous structures: the Forbidden City, home to the emperor; the Imperial City, home to officials and nobility; the Outer City, home to ordinary people; and the Temple of Heaven, one of China's most ornate religious buildings. According to Chinese art historian Ann Paludan, the Temple of Heaven was a symbol of one of Ming China's most important beliefs—that "all power, and hence all good, flows from a . . . Heaven transmitted through the emperor with his Mantle of Heaven."[27] The temple was where the emperor donned his ceremonial mantle, or robe, and prayed on behalf of the people for such things as a good harvest and blessings for the empire. Yongle also commissioned a series of imperial tombs in a valley 30 miles (48 km) northwest of Beijing. The tombs, which still stand today, are palatial and as well stocked as apartments, reflecting the belief that it was important to treat the dead as extravagantly as one treated the living.

Although today the most recognized of Yongle's legacies are his monuments and buildings, he also led five campaigns against the Mongols. And he commissioned six ship expeditions with the goal of establishing trade and diplomatic connections with Africa, Indonesia, and beyond.

The Forbidden City

The Forbidden City contained the private residence of the emperor, his extended family, and thousands of attendants. It contained a three-story theater, gardens, lakes, pavilions, parks, and paths. In the Pavilion of the Ceremony of Purification, the floor was carved into a 1-foot-deep (.3 m) stone stream that ran like a maze past picnickers. Visitors placed empty wine cups into the stream, where they floated away to be refilled and floated back to guests. The Forbidden City also had libraries, temples, and halls and palaces with such names as the Hall of Supreme Harmony and the Palace of Earthly Tranquility.

Both the ships and the expeditions were enormous. Estimates of the ships' lengths range from 385 feet (117 m) long to 440 feet (134 m) long. Some historians believe they may have been the largest wooden ships ever built. And if the ships were impressive, the expeditions were even more so. The first expedition in 1405, led by Admiral Zheng He, consisted of 317 ships and 27,387 sailors. The expeditions stopped in India and sailed to the Middle East, stopping at Jidda in what is now Saudi Arabia, and extended down the east African coast as far as Malindi in present-day Kenya. Zheng's ships came home in 1414 laden with exotic goods, spices, and the first giraffe the Chinese had ever seen.

Ming Defenses

The expansiveness of the early Ming Dynasty ended with Yongle. In the face of Mongol aggression at the border, later Ming rulers focused more on defense than on exploration. But the constant threat of Mongol invasions on the northern border led to what is perhaps the Ming's greatest monument: the Great Wall of China. Although many walls

The Great Wall of China, started in an earlier era, is most closely associated with the Ming Dynasty. Millions of peasants built the Ming wall, which separated China from the Mongols of the north.

had been built over nearly two thousand years of Chinese history, the Ming wall is perhaps the best known and the most intact of all previous walls. It was built with the forced labor of millions of peasants and ultimately stood at a length of 13,000 miles (20,922 km). The Great Wall separated China from the Mongols to the north. If it did not stop them entirely, it at least slowed them down. Ultimately, it provided China with its most distinctive symbol of greatness but also of separateness from the outside world.

Over the next two centuries, from behind the relative safety of the Great Wall, China grew into an economic and urban power. Even though most people still lived in the countryside, China's urban areas began to develop, and regional industries began to thrive. According to historian Roberts, "Jingdezhen, the porcelain centre in Jiangxi, claimed to have a population in excess of one million. The local magistrate complained that the fires of its kilns were so bright and the sound of its pestles so noisy that he could not sleep. Hangzhou, the great centre of silk production, was a city of similar size."[28]

In 1572, Ming emperor Wan Li came to power, and during his nearly fifty-year reign, China saw its first transformation into the modern state it would later become. Wan Li oversaw a China transformed by new crops—maize, peanuts, and sweet potatoes—which led to a healthier population. Cash crops such as cotton, sugarcane, and tobacco led to greater revenues and opportunities for production. Whereas cotton spinning was a rural cottage industry, weaving became a big operation in urban centers. By 1621 about two hundred thousand looms were in operation in Shanghai, and a new merchant class was growing to handle sales and distribution of goods. At the beginning of the seventeenth century, 1.6 million shiploads of goods passed through Linqing, a city in northern China on the Grand Canal. With a new class of people coming into wealth, urban areas blossomed and art flourished, particularly literature. Advances in printing and publishing led to an explosion of novels, stories, and dramas as well as books about science, industry, medicine, and history.

As his long reign progressed, however, problems on the border, compounded by Wan Li's increasing extravagance, spelled the beginning of the end of Ming rule. By the time Wan Li's grandson Chongzhen ascended the throne in 1628, the Ming Dynasty was discredited and broken. By 1644 China's dynastic golden ages were over.

Chapter 5

What Is the Legacy of China's Ancient Dynasties?

Few tourists visiting China today would miss a tour of the Great Wall. Nor would they feel they had gotten a full understanding of China's dynastic history without seeing the massive terra-cotta army in first emperor Qin Shi Huangdi's tomb. Selected segments of China's dynastic history are alive and well—complete with historical reenactments—for tourists to see and experience.

But not all of China's ancient dynastic legacies are as easy to glimpse in a short visit. Some are more subtle and lie at the very heart of how China functions as a nation. Other legacies are visible in the faces of the people, rural and urban, who work in China's fields and factories. And finally, China's ancient dynastic legacy is most evident in the land itself, in the way China's geography has been shaped and shifted over millennia.

Invention and Innovation

China's dynasties were among the wealthiest families the world has ever known. They lived lives of extreme privilege, surrounded by luxuries that their subjects could never even imagine. The homes and palaces of China's earliest dynasties, though modest by the standards of the rulers that followed, were as elaborate as any buildings of the time. Historian Bamber Gascoigne describes the rammed-earth structures that made up the homes of one of China's earliest dynasties: In the Great City of the Shang, "the foundations and lower walls of the more important buildings were made of the same pounded earth, with a wooden structure of pillars and perhaps a thatched roof above them. By contrast, the ordinary citizens lived in holes in the ground."[29]

Although the wealth of China's rulers generally did not filter down to the lower classes, the dynasties benefitted the population—and the world—in other ways. Under dynastic rule China supported many intellectual and technological achievements. Examples include the discovery of pi and negative numbers, which changed the world's understanding of mathematics. Paper, silk, printing and books, gunpowder and fireworks all have their origins in the era of China's dynasties. Gunpowder, developed around 850 CE, is thought to have spread from China through Europe by way of the Mongol invasions during the thirteenth century. By the fifteenth century gunpowder was starting to be used broadly in warfare. And by the 1600s gunpowder-propelled artillery dominated battles throughout the world. In fact, the European conquests of North and South America and Africa would not have been possible without the advantages that gunpowder gave colonial powers.

China's dynastic wealth also supported some of the world's most amazing and enduring examples of buildings and public works. The Great Wall of China, the Grand Canal, and enormous palaces are obvious examples of the magnificence and ingenuity of Chinese dynasties. More important, however, is the impact that China's dynasties have had on the structure of government throughout the world. The world's first bureaucracies—highly structured administrations—rose from early Chinese dynasties. Today this structure is seen not only in China but also in governments throughout the world.

Administration

Chinese dynasties unified a nation by conquering or bringing together dozens of ethnic groups and hundreds, if not thousands, of nation-states, cities, and villages. Even as these were absorbed into the empire, distinctions remained. Modern China consists of twenty-three provinces, four municipalities, five autonomous regions, and two special

Hoping to experience some sense of ancient China, hundreds of tourists walk on the Great Wall every day. Monuments are one legacy of China's ancient dynasties; how China functions as a modern nation is another.

administrative regions, each with roots reaching into China's rich dynastic history. How these different segments are organized and administered is one of the legacies of the dynastic era.

Dynasties administered the vast empire by standardizing language, laws, roads, and measurements. They created ways of managing public works projects and labor. And they found ways to collect taxes from citizens from every corner of the country. Each dynasty had its own way of maintaining control of its far-flung empire, both militarily and administratively, and many of these organizational traits are visible in China's bureaucratic system today.

One example in China's modern bureaucracy is the system of household registration. The modern *hukou* household registration system harkens back to similar registrations from as long ago as the Qin Dynasty. Qin registrations allowed the government to track residences, which gave China the ability to collect taxes and demand labor from each resident of a household. Today, according to the US Congressional-Executive Commission on China, "the Chinese *hukou* system has categorized citizens according to both place of residence and eligibility for certain socioeconomic benefits. Authorities issue citizens [urban or rural agricultural] *hukou* identification through a registration process administered by local authorities. Parents pass their *hukou* status to their children."[30] *Hukou* are inherited, along with the social identities and challenges that go with them. Thus, although people migrate from the country to the city, they cannot change their *hukou*. Many urban dwellers do not have urban *hukou*, which leaves them vulnerable to discrimination in accessing services such as schools and housing for their families. The *hukou* system is currently under reform, and the Chinese government is increasing urban *hukou* allotments to more closely match urban migration.

The present and past also connect in China's system of education and civil service examinations. In the Song Dynasty, for example, civil service job candidates took exams over and over, hoping for a higher grade to achieve a better job. The examinations offered a way to advance regardless of family wealth and status. The same can be seen today in China's system of college admissions, in which students with the highest scores on the national exam advance to college.

Colonization and Expansion

Although China's dynasties left legacies that have impacted the nation as a whole, some dynasties have left legacies at the provincial level as well. Each province has its own ancient history, often as the seat of a particular kingdom that was long ago conquered and incorporated into China by a ruling dynasty. And each of the five autonomous regions—minority-dominated regions with some degree of self-rule—has a story as the ancestral home of a distinct ethnic group, reflecting China's early expansion.

Chinese migrants, often called ethnic Han Chinese, under orders from dynasties throughout China's history, pushed out from central China to the west and north, south and east. Sometimes they moved

Dragons and fireworks are part of a celebration in China's capital of Beijing. China's dynasties gave the world many innovations including gunpowder and fireworks, paper, silk, printing, and a new understanding of mathematics.

with the support of the military. Sometimes an emperor would command groups of farmers to migrate in order to establish farming colonies in a particular area. Wherever and whenever they migrated, they shared their literate farming culture with the cultures they came in contact with, overwhelming other cultures throughout the region until Han Chinese culture became the dominant culture throughout the region. For example, according to geographer Robert B. Marks,

> That Ming Emperor Hongwu had a strong drive to colonize the southwest with [ethnic] Han Chinese migrants and officials is apparent, and the motivating forces included security

against Mongols and Tibetans, access to strategic raw materials, in particular silver and copper but other minerals and natural resources as well, and taxes from settling [ethnic] Han Chinese soldier-farmers on "uninhabited land."[31]

Colonizing a region by moving in and farming was an expansion tactic used by the Han Dynasty in the northwest, the Tang Dynasty in Sichuan, and the Song Dynasty in Lingnan.

Agricultural expansion into previously uncultivated lands, ordered by imperial leaders, is important today not only because it allowed Chinese culture to expand but because it also dramatically changed ecosystems throughout China. In the Ordos region of northern China, in an arid desert surrounded by a loop of the Yellow River, Ming Dynasty leaders sent colonists to transform Mongol grazing land into farmland. Colonists also resettled land in the southwest, with the help of tax credits, tools, and seeds supplied by Ming leaders. Once there, the settlers chopped down forests and plowed the land under with oxen and iron plows. Between 1385 and 1390, thirty thousand Chinese settlers cleared the age-old diverse ecosystems of the southwest and turned forests into farmland to grow grain. Today China's landscape, once covered with forests, is largely agricultural, impacting China's climate, watersheds, and its ability to filter pollutants in an increasingly industrial nation.

Ethnic Diversity

China's ethnic history is one of conquest, assimilation, and separatism. Although some ethnic groups assimilated, others remained separate. Today China is a multiethnic nation unified under the culture and Mandarin language of the Han Chinese ethnic group. But the other cultures and nations incorporated into a unified China did not disappear. Instead, they continue to live throughout the nation, particularly in China's five autonomous regions. Whereas the Han majority makes up more than 92 percent of the Chinese population, the remaining 8 percent is made up of the Manchu, Hui, Miao, Uyghur, Mongol, Tugia, Tibetan, Buyei Zhuang, Korean, and Tujia ethnic groups.

Confucian Ideals and Dynasty Dramas

Although the founders of the modern Chinese state rejected Confucianism, today some in China are rediscovering the values of Confucian thought. The *New York Times* reports that many people, from government advisers to television critics, are exploring what Confucian ideals might mean to a new Chinese society:

> China's new day in the economic sun is clouded somewhat by a spiraling crime rate, unemployment, corruption, and an increasing wealth gap—social ills that have many people looking to the ancient wisdom of Confucius for solutions. Kang Xiaoguang, social policy adviser to former premier Zhu Rongji, is one of them. Kang argues it is vital for China to rediscover its cultural tradition, especially the Confucian values he believes can rebuild the country's moral and social standards.

Television programs, popular throughout China, are also incorporating Confucianism into their story lines. According to the *New York Times*,

> Chinese television drama, particularly the costume dramas set during the dynasty era, has been at the forefront in articulating political and legal principles based on the Confucian influenced traditional Chinese culture. In its effort to engage the audiences who are fed up with rampant political corruption and the society's loss of moral grounding, dynasty drama has presented exemplary emperors of by-gone dynasties.

And while such dramas drive considerable debate as to what China's modern values should be, Confucianism is still a part of the conversation.

Ying Zhu, "The Confucian Tradition and Chinese Television Today," *New York Times*. www .nytimes.com.

China is home to fifty-five distinct ethnic minority groups who compose 8 percent of the population. These groups, however, occupy 50 to 60 percent of China's territory and have limited self-rule. Like the rest of the population, however, they must answer to China's central government.

China's ethnic minorities are Chinese citizens, but, in addition to speaking Mandarin, a Han Chinese language, they speak their own languages and have long, proud histories. The Nei Monggol autonomous region, for example, is in an area now known as Inner Mongolia. On the other side of the border is the nation of Mongolia. From these regions, five hundred years ago, came Genghis Khan and his descendants, who ultimately ruled China as the Yuan Dynasty. In the northwestern regions of China, the Uyghur Muslim minority is proud of its historical place as a stop on the Silk Road. And Manchu minorities live in China's northeast. There they maintained their traditional connections to nature through their involvement in forestry in the mountains of Manchuria during and after the fall of their Qing Dynasty, which ended during the twentieth century.

Even today China's ethnic minorities maintain many of their traditional values and practices. According to historians Hsin-Mei Chuang and Matthias Messmer, among the Miao ethnic minority in western Hunan Province, traditional rituals have been revived and embraced in recent years: "On market days, mothers often bring their toddlers to elderly women who perform blessing rituals using eggs specially prepared in big iron pans in quiet alleys. In addition, a few stands specializing in more alternative services, such as 'scientific fortune-telling,' . . . create a colorful spectacle."[32]

Perhaps because of their adherence to traditions, many ethnic minorities have faced discrimination among China's majority Han population. Miao women were once seen as witches, for example. As Messmer and Chuang explain, the

> Han majority ethnic group in China believed the Miao, especially the women, to be practitioners of witchcraft using venomous insects [called gu] which were abundant in this

lush, hilly, humid area. Stories were widespread of Han Chinese travelers being tortured or succumbing to gu-related diseases after abandoning their Miao lovers. Lonely, elderly Miao women were often suspected of employing sorcery against innocent victims.[33]

Some discrimination continues today. Many Miao in rural areas are so desperately poor that they migrate to cities in search of work in factories. Many of these migrants face discrimination in hiring, education, and housing, though China's recent reforms of the *hukou* system will allow many to receive equal rights as registered urban dwellers.

Keeping Traditions Alive

Although much has changed in China's modernized economy, in many areas the traditions and industries that began in dynastic times continue today. In the mountains of Manchuria, for example, where the Manchu ethnic group has traditionally gathered medicinal herbs, a thriving trade in the medicinal root ginseng continues to be an important part of the regional economy. Seeing how their ancient livelihood can provide a living in modern China is also a source of pride for the Manchu ethnic group.

Traditional arts, long a part of minority cultural identity, continue today in villages as a way to supplement farming income. In Hebei and Shaanxi Provinces, puppet making and the art of shadow puppetry began as early as the Han Dynasty. Hebei marionettes are intricately carved, painted, and dressed wooden puppets pulled by as many as a dozen strings. Many puppet plays concern nearly forgotten stories of Chinese history, and elderly performers work hard to transmit tales to modern audiences more used to television than folk art.

Ethnic minority craftsmen keep traditions alive to maintain their cultural identity. These traditional crafts and industries have also taken on an important economic role in impoverished rural areas, giving artisans additional income. Often these crafts were major industries in dynastic times, but today they continue on a very small scale. Since the Tang Dynasty, for example, Bai minority stone carvers have been creating monuments for everything from the original Forbidden City to contemporary private homes and cemeteries. Today many Bai artisans make a better living as stone carvers than they can as farmers. In Shanxi Province, beekeeping continues as a small-scale tradition, and in Hainan Province farmers collect latex from rubber trees for sale to factories. Other crafts, such as paper making and silk production, continue as a way to hang on to traditions while providing a small income. These crafts and industries, a legacy from ancient times, help rural Chinese survive in an often harsh modern economy.

A 2014 performance of traditional shadow puppets attracts the attention of spectators in Nanjing, the capital of Jiangsu Province. The art of shadow puppetry began in the Han Dynasty and continues on special occasions to this day.

Chinese Agriculture and Sustainability

China's landscape has changed over three thousand years from a land of forests and rivers, swamps and marshes, to a nation of small-scale agriculture and industry. Nevertheless, Chinese farming practices have been remarkably sustainable, says geographer Robert B. Marks:

> Land that was cleared for farms two thousand years ago is still farmed, and swamps and marshes that were drained and enclosed in polders [tracts of lowland protected by dikes] a thousand years ago still produce rice. Historically, Chinese farmers attained that productivity and maintained the viability of their farmland by regular and extensive recycling of nutrients lost to the soil.

Traditional farming practices, begun in the age of dynasties, kept the land productive.

By the twentieth and twenty-first centuries, however, some of China's farmland began losing its vitality. According to Marks,

> The combination of China's very long history of environmental degradation, coupled with the vast amounts of industrial and chemical fertilizer pollutants released into the land, water and air over the past thirty years may have created a situation in which China's natural environment has progressively lost its resilience and ability to recover from the damages inflicted by humans.

Robert B. Marks, *China: Its Environment and History*. Lanham, MD: Rowman and Littlefield, 2012, p. 335.

Silver Mining

China's imperial court represented one of the world's first great markets for trade of goods. This meant that dynasties often had an environmental impact far beyond the nation's borders. To supply imperial building projects—from the palaces and tombs of the Qin Dynasty to the summer palaces of the Yuan and the grandeur of the Ming Forbidden City—China's forests fell at a rate far faster than they could be replanted. Desire for exotic products such as timber, silver, and, later, sandalwood and furs sent Chinese traders far afield, pulling resources from every continent to fill imperial coffers.

Silver became especially valuable in the 1400s, when the paper money used by the Song and Yuan Dynasties fell into disfavor. The government began collecting silver as payment for taxes, and the Chinese economy began to be based on a silver currency. According to geographer Robert B. Marks, China's economy was so enormous and "the demand for silver so great that Ming China was soon importing vast quantities of silver from Japan, and, after the discovery of the New World, and its sources of silver, historians estimate that as much as one-half to two-thirds of all the silver extracted from the New World from 1500–1800 wound up in China."[34]

Chinese domestic silver mines were environmental disaster areas during the 1400s due to the simultaneous mining of cinnabar, a mineral containing mercury, which was used to help extract silver from rock. One Chinese critic of the mines, writing at the height of the industry, described the effects of mercury poisoning on the men who pulled cinnabar from rivers in the 1400s for use in the silver industry:

> With pans and pipes, they strain to gather a few fragments from the river. For many, standing in the river has caused their toes to rot and fall off, though the water they stand in is clear; their eyes are red and filled with tears, though their pupils have suffered irreparable damage. Because of the mining, the water appears red, and the clothing worn by the miners is stained red.[35]

Deforestation

Another important result of the changing, stretching marketplace was an increased demand for lumber—and the consequent deforestation. In remote areas of China, felled trees were floated down rivers for sale in cities that were springing up on the Grand Canal. People in cities wanted wood for houses, furniture, and other products. And no one wanted them more than the noblemen of the dynastic courts. In Manchuria and other mountainous areas, old-growth timber was cut, brought to market in Beijing, and used to create imperial dwellings. As the forests were depleted and the ground denuded, the hillsides grew unstable. During the rainy season, water pouring down the bare slopes carried dirt with it. Rivers were clogged with debris.

Before 1194 the Huai River valley was a prosperous agricultural region. Irrigation ditches and canals created during the Han Dynasty allowed farmers to grow rice in abundance as well as catch fish and clams. As the slopes of mountains were deforested, however, massive amounts of soil washed down hillsides, clogging rivers and canals and making crop irrigation difficult. From 1400 to 1900, the valley saw 350 floods, each bringing sterile sand rather than rich soil to farmlands. The dynastic appetite for wood caused a drastic change in many of China's ecosystems and water systems.

The military conquests of China's dynasties further impacted the environment. When the Yao people of the wild mountains of western Guangxi rebelled in 1465, for example, the minister of war responded by setting fire to the forests, cutting down all the trees, and driving roads through the hills to find the rebels. And when the Mongols conquered China to found the Yuan Dynasty, they laid waste to whatever land lay before them. Because the Mongols were pastoral people, they destroyed farmland. No matter who was fighting, the land bore the brunt of the damage. Such ecological warfare had an impact on China's environment. The scars of centuries of fighting and deforestation are visible today in landscapes that are deforested and eroded.

A Living Legacy

The historical legacy of China's dynasties is evident in monuments and markets, government structures, and Chinese arts, crafts and environments. Today, as China's people strive to create a modern society, they are never far from the China of their ancestors. They see China's ancient dynasties in the walls of their villages and the ethnicities of their neighbors. They experience it in the agriculture of the countryside and the bureaucracy of their cities. They perceive it in the expansion of Chinese trade throughout the world and in the annual celebrations of the New Year that have brought them together as a people for more than forty-seven hundred years. Ancient Chinese dynasties are alive and well, a legacy that lives on.

Source Notes

Introduction: The Defining Characteristics of the Ancient Chinese Dynasties

1. J.A.G. Roberts, *A History of China,* 3rd ed. London: Palgrave Mac-Millan, 2011, p. xiii.

2. Quoted in Ann Paludan, *Chronicle of the Chinese Emperors: The Reign-By-Reign Record of the Rulers of Imperial China.* London: Thames & Hudson, 2009, p. 187.

3. Su Shuyang, *A Reader on China: An Introduction to China's History, Culture, and Civilization.* Shanghai: Better Link, 2007, p. 68.

Chapter One: What Conditions Led to the Ancient Chinese Dynasties?

4. Quoted in Keith Buchanan, Charles P. Fitzgerald, and Colin A. Ronan, *China: The Land and the People; The History, the Art, and the Science.* New York: Crown, 1980, p. 55.

5. Su, *A Reader on China,* pp. 11–12.

6. Quoted in Patricia Buckley Ebrey, *Chinese Civilization: A Sourcebook.* New York: Free, 1993, pp. 3–4.

7. Quoted in Chinese Cultural Studies, "The Mandate of Heaven, Selections from the *Shu Jing* (The Classic of History) (6th Cent. BCE)," City University of New York, Brooklyn College. http://acc6.its.brooklyn.cuny.edu.

Chapter Two: Unity Under Empire: The Qin and Han Dynasties

8. Lin Handa and Cao Yuzhang, trans. Yawtsong Lee, *Tales from 5,000 Years of Chinese History,* vol. 1. Shanghai: Better Link, 2010, p. 56.

9. Quoted in Roberts, *A History of China,* p. 21.

10. Lin and Cao, *Tales from 5,000 Years of Chinese History,* p. 57.
11. Quoted in Julia Lovell, *The Great Wall: China Against the World, 1000 BC to AD 2000.* New York: Grover, 2006, p. 50.
12. Quoted in Jacques Gernet, *A History of Chinese Civilization.* Cambridge, UK: Cambridge University Press, 1982, p. 162.
13. Quoted in Ebrey, *Chinese Civilization,* p. 65.

Chapter Three: The Rise of the Northern Dynasties
14. Gernet, *A History of Chinese Civilization,* p. 192.
15. Su, *A Reader on China,* p. 80.
16. Roberts, *A History of China,* pp. 48–49.
17. Roberts, *A History of China,* p. 50.
18. Quoted in Jonathan Fryer, *The Great Wall of China.* London: New English Library, 1975, p. 15.
19. Bamber Gascoigne, *The Dynasties of China: A History.* New York: Carroll and Graf, 2003, pp. 140–41.
20. Francesco Balducci Pegolotti, *Practica della Mercatura,* Allen Evans, ed., in *Cathay and the Way Thither,* vol. III, Henry Yule and Henri Cordier, trans. and eds. London: Hakluyt Society, 1916. https://depts.washington.edu/silkroad/texts/pegol.html.
21. Asia for Educators, "The Mongols in World History," Columbia University, 2004. http://afe.easia.columbia.edu.

Chapter Four: The Golden Ages of Dynastic Rule
22. Roberts, *A History of China,* p. 52.
23. Roberts, *A History of China,* p. 63.
24. Quoted in Roberts, *A History of China,* p. 64.
25. Quoted in Gascoigne, *The Dynasties of China,* p. 117.
26. Quoted in Gascoigne, *The Dynasties of China,* p. 126.
27. Quoted in Lin and Cao, *Tales from 5,000 Years of Chinese History,* p. 168.
28. Roberts, *A History of China,* pp. 126–27.

Chapter Five: What Is the Legacy of China's Ancient Dynasties?

29. Gascoigne, *The Dynasties of China,* pp. 22–23.

30. Congressional-Executive Commission on China, "Special Topic Paper: China's Household Registration System: Sustained Reform Needed to Protect China's Rural Migrants," March 29, 2006. www .cecc.gov.

31. Robert B. Marks, *China: Its Environment and History.* Lanham, MD: Rowman and Littlefield, 2012, p. 180.

32. Matthias Messmer and Hsin-Mei Chuang, *China's Vanishing Worlds: Countryside, Traditions, and Cultural Spaces.* Cambridge, MA: MIT Press, 2013, p. 108.

33. Messmer and Chuang, *China's Vanishing Worlds,* p. 108.

34. Marks, *China: Its Environment and History,* p. 182.

35. Quoted in Marks, *China: Its Environment and History,* p. 183.

Important People of the Ancient Chinese Dynasties

Confucius: An itinerant philosopher who believed in honesty, enterprise, and filial piety. His teachings continue to influence China in modern times.

Genghis Khan: A Mongol leader who, with his descendants, conquered China and much of the rest of the world. His Mongol empire extended from Europe, through India, to China and beyond.

Marco Polo: An Italian merchant who was among the first Europeans to live in China. His writings, published long after he returned to Italy, influenced European ideas about China for centuries.

Qin Shi Huangdi: The first emperor of China. He unified China militarily and standardized and systematized China's roads, currency, language, writing, and measurements.

Matteo Ricci: A Jesuit monk who visited China during the late 1500s and stayed, learning Chinese in order to spread Christianity and writing about what he observed.

Yongle: The Ming Dynasty emperor who commissioned the building of many great monuments, including the Forbidden City and parts of the Great Wall.

Zhang Qian: A civilian official sent to make military contacts outside of China around 138 BCE. Instead, he established commercial connections, opening up China to the beginnings of the thriving trade known as the Silk Road.

Zheng He: An admiral in the Ming navy. Emperor Yongle commissioned him to take six voyages of discovery to extend Chinese markets into India, the Middle East, and Africa.

For Further Research

Books

Bamber Gascoigne, *The Dynasties of China: A History*. New York: Carroll and Graf, 2003.

Cindy Jenson-Elliott, *The Great Wall of China*. San Diego: ReferencePoint, 2014.

John Keay, *China: A History*. New York: Basic, 2009.

Lin Handa and Cao Yuzhang, *Tales from 5,000 Years of Chinese History*. Shanghai: Better Link, 2010.

Julia Lovell, *The Great Wall: China Against the World, 1000 BC to AD 2000*. New York: Grover, 2006.

Robert B. Marks, *China: Its Environment and History*. Lanham, MD: Rowman and Littlefield, 2012.

Matthias Messmer and Hsin-Mei Chuang, *China's Vanishing Worlds: Countryside, Traditions, and Cultural Spaces*. Cambridge, MA: MIT Press, 2013.

J.A.G. Roberts, *A History of China,* 3rd ed. London: Palgrave MacMillan, 2011.

Harold M. Tanner, *China: A History*. Indianapolis: Hackett, 2009.

Websites

Asia for Educators (http://afe.easia.columbia.edu). Hosted by Columbia University, this website contains readings, maps, curriculum resources, and insights into Chinese history and culture.

British Museum, "China: Tang Dynasty (AD 618–906)" (www.british museum.org/explore/highlights/article_index/c/china_tang_dynasty _ad_618-90.aspx). The British Museum is one of the world's premier museums for archaeology and anthropology. It contains extensive artifacts collected from around the world, including many from ancient China.

Classical Historiography of Chinese History (www.princeton.edu /~classbib/). This website contains bibliographies and resources such as maps and information about ancient Chinese history.

Congressional-Executive Commission on China (www.cecc.gov/publi cations/issue-papers/cecc-special-topic-paper-chinas-household-regis tration-system-sustained). This website has a variety of information about current topics of interest on Chinese policy and reforms. One article in particular, the "Special Topic Paper: China's Household Registration System: Sustained Reform Needed to Protect China's Rural Migrants," offers contemporary information on an issue important to Chinese people today: household registrations.

Minneapolis Institute of Arts (www.artsmia.org/art-of-asia/history /chinese-dynasty-guide.cfm). This website offers a guide to its *Art of Asia* exhibits, including art and artifacts.

Society for Anglo-Chinese Understanding (www.sacu.org). The Society for Anglo-Chinese Understanding promotes friendship between British and Chinese people. Its website contains a Chinese history chart as well as information about such things as Chinese inventions, Chinese kites, and more.

UNESCO World Heritage Sites (http://whc.unesco.org). This website is the official guide to World Heritage Sites throughout the world. World Heritage Sites are places that the United Nations Educational, Scientific and Cultural Organization has deemed of great value to the human race. A number of sites exist in China, including the Great Wall of China.

UShistory.org, "Shang Dynasty—China's First Recorded History" (www.ushistory.org/civ/9b.asp). UShistory.org is a website that explores and explains many aspects of history, both world history and US history, including the history of the Shang Dynasty.

Index

Picture Credits

Large Longquan celadon tripod censer with Japanese parcel-gilt metal cover (ceramic) (see also 349496), Chinese School, Southern Song Dynasty (11th–12th Century)/Museum of Art, Santa Barbara, California, CA, USA/Photo © Christie's Images/Bridgeman Images: 59

Building the Great Wall of China (gouache on paper), McBride, Angus (1931–2007) / Private Collection / © Look and Learn / Bridgeman Images: 64

About the Author

Cindy Jenson-Elliott is the author of fifteen books of nonfiction. She lives with her family in Southern California.